Illinois Institute of Technology

THE CAMPUS GUIDE

Illinois Institute of Technology

AN ARCHITECTURAL TOUR BY

Franz Schulze

WITH PHOTOGRAPHS BY

Richard Barnes

FOREWORD BY

Lew Collens

Princeton Architectural Press

NEW YORK | 2005

Princeton Architectural Press
37 East Seventh Street
New York, New York 10003

For a free catalog of books, call 1.800.722.6657.
Visit our web site at www.papress.com.

All images by Richard Barnes unless otherwise noted.

Photo credits:
pp. vi–v: IIT Residence Halls © Chicago Historical Society, HB 18783-D, photographer Hedrich Blessing
pp. viii–ix: Alumni Memorial Hall © Chicago Historical Society, HB-9767-A, photographer Hedrich Blessing
pp. xvi, 1, 2, 3, 4, 5, 6, 8, 11, 29, 43, 48, 64, 72 top, 75, 79, 94: Reproduced by permission of University Archives, Paul V. Galvin Library, Illinois Institute of Technology, Chicago. IIT has made every reasonable attempt to identify owners of copyright. Errors or omissions will be corrected in subsequent editions.
p. 8: © Miles Boone Photography, reproduced by permission of IIT
pp. 14, 36, 37, 65, 66, 67, 71, 72 bottom, 74, 77, 83, 84, 89, 92 top: © Nicola Bednarek
p. 26: © Mark Stevens
p. 27: © Bogunita Robinson
p. 76: © David Hovey, Architect

Series editor: Nancy Eklund Later
Series concept: Dennis Looney
Project editor: Nicola Bednarek
Layout: Nicola Bednarek
Maps: Jane Sheinman

Special thanks to: Nettie Aljian, Janet Behning, Megan Carey, Penny (Yuen Pik) Chu, Russell Fernandez, Jan Haux, Clare Jacobson, John King, Mark Lamster, Linda Lee, John McGill, Katharine Myers, Lauren Nelson, Molly Rouzie, Scott Tennent, Jennifer Thompson, Joseph Weston, and Deb Wood of Princeton Architectural Press —Kevin C. Lippert, publisher

Library of Congress Cataloging-in-Publication Data
Schulze, Franz, 1927–
   Illinois Institute of Technology : the campus guide : an architectural tour / by Franz Schulze ; with photographs by Richard Barnes ; foreword by Lew Collens.—1st ed.
      p. cm.
   Includes bibliographical references and index.
   ISBN 1-56898-482-0 (alk. paper)
   1. Illinois Institute of Technology. I. Barnes, Richard, 1953– II. Title.
   T171.I25S38 2005
   727'.3'0977311—dc22
                                    2004024446

Printed and bound in China

CONTENTS

This book is intended for visitors, alumnae/i, and students who wish to have an insider's look at the campus of Illinois Institute of Technology, from the Romanesque-revival Main Building of 1891, to Mies van der Rohe's International Style masterpieces, to the new campus center by Rem Koolhaas of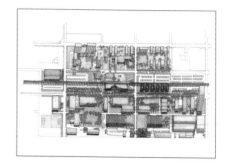
2003. The guide starts with an introduction that gives a brief overview of the university's history, followed by an architectural walking tour that leads around the campus with descriptions and photographs of each building or site. A biographical essay on Mies provides the reader with more information on the architect's life and buildings.

Visitors are welcome to tour the IIT campus:
To arrange a tour, please contact the campus information desk at 312.567.3700. For more information on IIT, please visit www.iit.edu.

Acknowledgments

My special thanks to Edward Windhorst, Chicago architect and graduate of Illinois Institute of Technology, for his exceptional knowledge of the campus and its architecture; to Catherine Bruck, IIT university archivist, for her understanding of the university's history; and to Nicola Bednarek, for her thoughtful editing.

Franz Schulze

Robert F. Carr Memorial Chapel

Truly great architecture reflects, supports, and enhances the mission and spirit of a university. This is evident at Illinois Institute of Technology, where our intellectual and physical environment work together to create a setting in which leadership, entrepreneurship, and invention thrive. Throughout this book you will learn more about our landmark Mies buildings and our award-winning new campus center and residence hall—but first I would like to introduce you to the people and programs at IIT that inspire and enliven them.

Since its inception in 1890, IIT has prepared students for leadership in an increasingly complex and culturally diverse global workplace. Now more than ever, that preparation requires an interprofessional approach as science, technology, business, law, and other disciplines intersect to create the policies and discoveries that will shape our future.

IIT's legacy of excellence in interprofessional education has attracted students from all over the globe. Last year, students from more than a hundred countries came to study a wide variety of fields, such as engineering, science, business, law, architecture, design, psychology, and finance. These students are some of the best and brightest in the world.

All of this talent converges in an environment that focuses on cutting-edge science and technology. Our signature Interprofessional Projects Program (IPRO) unites students and faculty of different disciplines to solve real-world problems—with hands-on experience that uniquely prepares students for their future careers. Through these IPROs, students have tackled projects in several dynamic fields: alternative energy sources, including solar energy, hydrogen power, and wind turbines; improvements in medical and health care, including new wheelchair design, improved monitoring techniques for heart surgery, and better methods for collecting and analyzing blood samples; and enhanced living conditions in countries around the world from the Balkans to El Salvador.

This interprofessional approach is a common thread that runs through all of our programs. Our techno-business program is preparing leaders who understand the vital relationship between business and technology. Our biomedical engineering program is providing scientists with strong technical and engineering skills. Our Institute for Science, Law, and Technology is developing policy leaders who can address the complex issues in these interrelated fields. In every program, our faculty members are challenging students to transcend traditional disciplinary boundaries and explore the connections between them.

IIT actively collaborates with business, government, and other universities to provide our students with the best resources possible. Two prime examples of this team approach are our combined honors program in engineering and medicine with Rush Medical College and our neuroengi-neering program with the University of Chicago's Pritzker School of Medicine. These collaborative efforts offer our students an outstanding breadth and depth of knowledge and resources to ensure their success.

As our faculty members prepare students for future success, they are also busy making their own impact by taking discoveries from the laboratory into the real world. At IIT's Life Science Research and Development Park, faculty researchers are working at the forefront of cancer research, utilizing a $28-million grant from the National Cancer Institute to pioneer new methods of treating and preventing the disease. IIT researchers are develop-ing prostheses to provide vision to the blind, creating biosensors to enhance public healthcare and homeland security, and building hybrid electric vehi-cles to help reduce pollution and conserve energy. Our faculty and students are making discoveries that are changing how we live and work.

IIT students have gone on to become global leaders in govern-ment—from U.S. governors, senators, and judges to foreign prime ministers and presidents. Some have become inventors, such as Marty Cooper, who developed the cell phone, and Marvin Camras, who pioneered modern radio technology. Others have become architects who have provided the technical and artistic leadership responsible for many of Chicago's mag-nificent buildings as well as other important structures around the world. Our faculty list is no less distinguished, with three Nobel Prize winners, a National Medal of Technology recipient, and hundreds of other educators who have received honors and recognition for leadership and contributions to their fields.

As IIT invests in the extraordinary potential of our students and faculty, we are also dedicated to supporting our neighborhood. Our recent building additions and renovations and landscape architecture enhancements reflect our commitment to Chicago's revitalized South Side, and we continue to work closely with local government and organizations to build a vibrant community for all who live, work, and study here.

Ludwig Mies van der Rohe once called S. R. Crown Hall a "home of ideas and adventures." Today, our entire campus embodies this spirit and serves a primary function: to be an incubator for innovative thinking. I invite you to visit our campus, tour our buildings, and take some time to meet the future leaders, entrepreneurs, and inventors who are bringing Mies's vision of a flexible, open, and interactive learning environment to life every day. IIT is truly a place that is transforming lives and inventing the future.

Lew Collens
President, Illinois Institute of Technology

TOP: *Armour Flats*
BOTTOM: *Armour Mission*

LEFT: *Reverend Frank Wakely Gunsaulus*
RIGHT: *Philip Danforth Armour, Sr.*

Introduction

Illinois Institute of Technology has been an educational trailblazer since it emerged from the union of two earlier Chicago institutions, Lewis Institute and Armour Institute of Technology. Both preceding schools reflected their founders' desire to empower young people of limited means to lead more fulfilling lives. Today, IIT continues this legacy of quality academic preparation by offering a sophisticated technological education to students from around the world.

Armour Institute

Armour Institute took root in a sermon that Rev. Frank Wakely Gunsaulus delivered on Chicago's South Side in 1890. That day, Gunsaulus told his parishioners at Plymouth Congregational Church that a rapidly industrializing society—one being shaped by new technologies—depended on technicians for continued progress. If he had a million dollars, he said, he would create a school for young people who wished to train as technicians but could not otherwise afford to do so. Industrialist Philip Danforth Armour, Sr. (1832–1901) was in the audience that day, and after the service, Armour approached Gunsaulus. As it was later described, "The man who had the means grasped the man who had the vision, and together they made the dream come true."

The singular success of his meatpacking business, Armour & Co., had made Armour a wealthy man—wealthy enough by the 1880s to follow his philanthropic impulses. Armour supported the church where Rev.

Allen C. Lewis

Gunsaulus officiated as well as the Plymouth Mission School, which served the working people in its neighborhood. With the financial help of the Armour family the mission thrived, and a substantial brick and stone building designed by the ascendant Chicago architectural partnership of Daniel H. Burnham and John Wellborn Root opened in 1886 at the corner of Thirty-third Street and Armour Avenue (later Federal Street). During that same year, Philip Armour saw to the construction, at a cost of $1 million, of 194 apartments in an area bordered by Thirty-third, Thirty-fourth, Federal, and Dearborn streets. The complex, known as the Armour Flats, served upper-level employees of Armour & Co. and was regarded as among the finest group of apartments in the city. The Flats were largely demolished in the early twentieth century, but some of the remaining apartments were later taken over by Armour Institute for academic purposes.

The school's initial site was at the intersection of Thirty-third Street and Armour Avenue, just across from the mission. When Armour Institute opened its doors in 1893, its original program had two components: manual training for men, meant to produce mechanics and technicians, and domestic training for women. Gunsaulus altered this simple formula after traveling to Europe, where he witnessed the importance of professional-level instruction in engineering. He enlarged the scope of the school's program, and a Scientific Academy formed the heart of this revised curriculum. (In 1895, the school was renamed Armour Institute of Technology [AIT] to reflect its growing reputation for engineering.) In 1903, college level evening courses were added so that working students could also pursue a degree.

Lewis Institute

Meanwhile, Lewis Institute was beginning operations on Chicago's West Side. While its beginnings lacked the rhetorical flourish of Armour Institute's founding moments, it was born of an equally sincere commitment to help young people who would otherwise be unable to afford an education. Allen C. Lewis, a successful Chicago real estate investor, died in 1877 and left a sizeable estate with a mandate that it be used to create a technical

Lewis Institute, ca. 1895

school that would provide a college education to men and women. Within a generation, his bequest had grown to $1.6 million, which was a sustantial enough figure that the estate's trustees sought a charter. The motto "Science, Literature, Technology" was carved into the school's entrance, and those words effectively summarized the college's mission.

The school was structured in accordance with Lewis's specific directions: it provided a practical education that would enable its graduates to earn a living, and it offered a public library and reading room. Under the leadership of its first director, George Noble Carman, Lewis Institute initiated a four-year degree track as well as a two-year associate's degree, making it the first junior college in the United States. (In addition to being an eminently capable administrator, Carman helped establish the accreditation body that certifies American colleges and universities to this day.)

While the two institutions were in many ways alike, one notable difference was the composition of their respective student bodies. Armour Institute was a "street-car college" that primarily served working-class male students of Chicago's South Side. Lewis Institute, on the other hand, attracted students from across the spectrum of Chicago's immigrant population, as well as international students from India to China to the Philippines. Students took advantage of its citizenship classes, English courses, and commitment to religious tolerance and cultural exchange.

Mies van der Rohe (middle) with the architecture faculty, 1948

Illinois Institute of Technology

The hardships of the Great Depression in the 1920s and early 1930s threatened countless institutions throughout the country, and Lewis and Armour institutes were no exception. In the late 1930s, the two schools entered talks, and in 1939, they agreed to consolidate and form a new institution. By joining forces, they ensured the survival of their shared mission: empowering young people to lead independent, meaningful lives. When the combined boards of both schools met in July of 1940, they finalized the creation of the new Illinois Institute of Technology (IIT).

After World War II, Lewis Institute's buildings at Robey Street (now Damen Avenue) and Madison Street were sold to the City of Chicago, and the old Armour Campus on Chicago's South Side became home to IIT. At that time, it was comprised of a few nineteenth- and early twentieth-century structures, including Main Building, Machinery Hall, and a laboratory—the three oldest surviving buildings on campus today. Main and Machinery halls stand as notable examples of Romanesque revival architecture. Constructed of deep red brick and sandstone walls, red terra cotta and molded brick trim, and round arched windows and entrances, they received City of Chicago landmark status in 2003.

As impressive as these buildings were, it quickly became evident that the school would need to expand its campus facilities in order to accommodate the growing organization. Whether or not it was clear at the time,

View of the IIT campus, ca. 1940

IIT's need for growth would catalyze a new chapter not only in its own story, but in architectural history as well.

The Mies van der Rohe Years

Two years before the merger was finalized, AIT made a historic faculty appointment when it hired Ludwig Mies van der Rohe to serve as director of the department of architecture. The fifty-two-year-old German native, already an internationally renowned architect, arrived in Chicago in 1938. AIT welcomed him and two other Germans he had selected as faculty members, Ludwig Hilberseimer and Walter Peterhans. The three men had taught at the famed Bauhaus, the school of modern art and architecture that Mies headed from 1930 to 1934, before the Nazis forced it to close. A fourth man, John Barney Rodgers—an American alumnus of the Bauhaus who was fluent in German—joined as an administrative assistant to Mies. These additions to the faculty made it clear that AIT was adding considerable substance to its architecture program.

AIT eagerly provided a receptive environment to Mies, who was a pioneer of European modernism. His new curriculum required students to learn at a deliberate pace, beginning with the fundamentals of drawing and advancing to the study of materials and basic construction principles, and eventually to the design of complex buildings.

Within a year of Mies's arrival, AIT commissioned him to design an innovative master plan encompassing the entire campus. His new

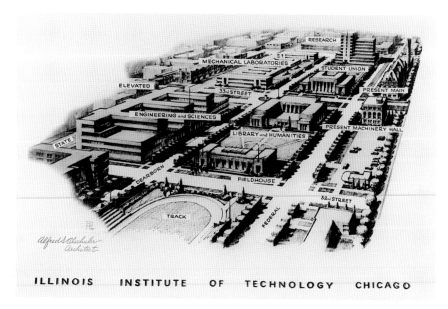

Plan for IIT, Alfred Alschuler, 1940

architectural curriculum would infuse this plan even as it shaped the very environment for it. Architecture and campus planning would signal an immense shift in the organization, the direction, and the very identity of the school.

When Mies arrived, he found a campus bordered by Thirty-first Street on the north, Thirty-fourth Street on the south, State Street on the east, and the New York Central Railroad tracks on the west. In the late 1930s, the administration bought up property adjacent to these buildings to make space for new construction.

In fact, Mies's was not the original master plan: one had been fashioned in 1937 by the Chicago firm of Holabird & Root; another plan was developed by Chicago architect and AIT trustee Alfred Alschuler as late as 1940—after Mies had begun work on his own plan. Both the Holabird & Root and Alschuler plans showed the influence of beaux-arts principles, while Mies's proposal was much closer to the image of modernity that Henry Heald, who was president of AIT from 1938 to 1939 and president of IIT from 1940 to 1952, envisioned for the university.

Before its final approval in 1941, the Mies master plan went through numerous phases, some of which included specific buildings—most notably the Library and Administration Building—that probably would have been among Mies's most impressive achievements if they had been built. By 1943, one of his designs, the Minerals and Metals Research Building, was complete, but it was not until 1945 that the building program began in earnest. Construction matched the heightened pace that overtook nearly all activities at IIT. Enrollment, which had fallen during World War II when

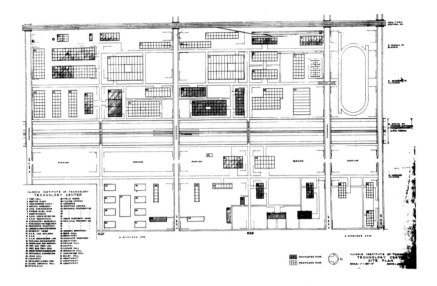

Plan for IIT, Mies van der Rohe, 1956 © Chicago Historical Society, HB-19108-A, photographer Hedrich Blessing

the armed forces claimed many otherwise eligible students, now rose at a rapid rate, and this surge necessitated the construction of Farr and Fowler residence halls in 1948. The Chicago office of Skidmore, Owings & Merrill designed both.

By 1950, ten new structures had gone up. Seven of these were by Mies. His approach was clear: IIT was rapidly transforming into a wholly modernist campus, and since the campus had grown to sixty-five acres, it was able to accommodate most of Mies's vision. IIT continued to buy land, razing derelict buildings and replacing them with a green, open landscape that could readily accept new structures. When Mies retired in 1958, the campus extended south to Thirty-fifth Street and had twenty-two Mies-designed buildings. These included three identically planned, nine-story apartment buildings for staff, faculty, and married students—named, respectively, for George Noble Carman (1953), Alex D. Bailey (1955), and James D. Cunningham (1955)—as well as the Robert F. Carr Memorial Chapel of St. Savior (1952), the Commons (1953), and S. R. Crown Hall (1956).

Crown Hall, whose column-free interior was conceived as the ideal home for the department of architecture, is widely considered the architect's finest work and was designated a National Historic Landmark in 2001. Mies was seventy-two when he retired from IIT, but his designs served as models for much of what was constructed during the 1960s by other architects. The Chicago office of Skidmore, Owings & Merrill—and specifically two of the firm's best-known partners—received a number of the building commissions. Walter Netsch was responsible for two buildings: the Grover M. Hermann

Hall (1961), which functioned as a student union, and the John Crerar and James S. Kemper libraries (1962), later the Paul V. Galvin Library. Both buildings echo Mies's Crown Hall, particularly in the use of plate girders to support their roofs.

Another partner, Myron Goldsmith, who had studied with Mies at IIT, was the lead designer of four buildings: Arthur Keating Hall, an athletic facility containing a gymnasium and pool (1966); Life Sciences Building (1966); Engineering I Building (1968); and Harold Leonard Stuart Building, built as the headquarters of the School of Business Administration (1971). All but Keating applied the architectural vocabulary of Mies's classroom buildings. The Chicago firm of Schmidt, Garden & Erikson also produced four structures indicative of Mies's influence: Armour Research Foundation Chemistry Research Building (1960); Institute of Gas Technology (IGT) Power Plant (1964); IGT Central Building (1965); and IIT Research Institute (IITRI) (1965).

Renewal Plans

The building boom ceased in 1971, and the campus remained relatively unchanged until the university, under the leadership of President Lewis Collens, revisited its campus master plan. In 1993, IIT convened a National Commission, consisting of highly respected outside leaders, trustees, and faculty. They began a review of the school's comprehensive academic, financial, and physical status.

First, the commission addressed the physical state of the main campus and its surrounding South Side community, since virtually everything else within its field of vision revolved around this issue. They proposed partnerships with private supporters and local, city, and state governments to pursue improved living and working conditions in the immediate vicinity of the campus.

The school's efforts quickly gained momentum. Early in 1995, the Urban Land Institute issued a study of IIT's development options, which included a possible relocation to the Chicago suburbs, and recommended strongly that IIT stay and leverage its South Side asset of land and buildings. Later that year, the IIT administration commissioned the architectural firm of Lohan Associates (headed by Dirk Lohan, an IIT trustee and Mies's grandson) to produce a main campus master plan that would transform IIT into an ideal place to study, live, and work.

The Board of Trustees approved the Lohan master plan in May 1996. In order to enhance the campus community, the plan made several major recommendations. It called for a new student union to be built at Thirty-third and State streets in the center of campus. Although Hermann Hall had long functioned as a student union, it was well removed from the

Aerial view of the IIT campus

LEFT: *Robert W. Galvin*
RIGHT: *Robert A. Pritzker*

student residences east of State Street and never fulfilled its purpose. The new facility would function as the social and aesthetic heart of the university and unify the disparate sides of campus. The master plan also recommended the creation of a historic district encompassing Mies's academic buildings as well as the restoration of these buildings and the surrounding landscape architecture. In addition, the plan recommended that the university fulfill Mies's original vision for IIT as a "campus in the park," which Mies and famed landscape architect and popular IIT instructor Alfred Caldwell had developed during the planning stages of the 1940s and 1950s. Much of their plan, which relied on a close relationship of buildings and plantings, had never been realized.

IIT soon received the means to fulfill even broader dreams of growth and renewal, both in terms of its campus and its curriculum. In November of 1996, President Collens announced a historic philanthropic gift to IIT. Trustees Robert W. Galvin and Robert A. Pritzker made a gift of $120 million—one of the largest in the history of American private education—structured around a challenge to IIT and its donors to match their contribution dollar-for-dollar. The gift encouraged the university's ambitious goals, including scholarship and faculty funding as well as sweeping physical improvements.

The Pritzker/Galvin Challenge initiated a new period of growth and renewal at IIT, and in 1997, the university launched the Richard H. Driehaus International Design Competition for its new campus center. Many of the world's leading architects participated, with five firms reaching

Landscape architect Alfred Caldwell (center) with students

the final phase: Peter Eisenman of New York; Zaha Hadid of London; Helmut Jahn of Chicago (in collaboration with Werner Sobek of Stuttgart); Rem Koolhaas of the Office of Metropolitan Architecture in Rotterdam; and Kazuyo Sejima and Ryue Nishizawa of Tokyo.

The jury unanimously awarded the commission to Pritzker Architecture Prize laureate Rem Koolhaas, who had succinctly addressed one of the key problems of the center's location—the adjacency to the elevated train tracks just east of State Street—with an innovative stainless steel–clad acoustical tube that encased the tracks. In addition to impressing the jury, the plan inspired financial support: the McCormick Tribune Foundation provided the lead gift for the construction of the Koolhaas design. A year later, the state of Illinois, under Governor George Ryan, followed suit with a grant to help finance construction of the tube. By 1999, campus beautification had begun in earnest, based on a landscaping master plan created in 1998 by the team of Michael Van Valkenburgh of Cambridge, Massachusetts, and Peter Lindsay Schaudt of Chicago. The City of Chicago, under Mayor Richard M. Daley, provided $7 million to transform the stretch of State Street from Thirtieth to Thirty-fifth streets into a "green corridor." The plan included narrowing the street from three to two lanes and planting five hundred trees.

State Street Village (left) with the tube encasing the train trucks over The McCormick Tribune Campus Center

Today, IIT has achieved most of the ambitious goals drawn up by the National Commission. The university has either met or is well on its way to meeting the recommendations outlined in the Lohan master plan: the Pritzker/Galvin Challenge campaign has concluded successfully a year ahead of schedule; extensive new landscape architecture has transformed the campus environment; The McCormick Tribune Campus Center, dedicated in 2003, serves as a vibrant new hub for student life; and State Street Village, a new residence complex designed by alumnus Helmut Jahn, opened in 2003.

A Modern Campus for a Modern University

IIT, which embraced modernism over sixty years ago, is home to some of Chicago's most daring new buildings. Architectural critics around the world have heralded The McCormick Tribune Campus Center, which is Koolhaas's first building constructed in the United States. With its bold colors, high-tech materials, and lively angles, it offers a visual tribute to the university's new energy and direction even as it pays homage to Mies. State Street Village, the high-tech student residence, is set across the street from the new campus center. This acclaimed project consists of three two-wing units constructed of concrete clad in steel and aluminum and joined with generous sheaths of glass.

At the same time that the university has added new buildings, it has also refocused on the renewal of its historic Mies campus. In November 2002, IIT launched its Mies van der Rohe Society, dedicated to the revitalization of the core Mies-designed buildings. In addition to preserving the architectural integrity of the structures, the society is also ensuring that IIT preserves Mies's vision and that the buildings continue to meet the needs of IIT's students for generations to come. Currently, the Society is focusing on Crown Hall, Wishnick Hall, and Carr Memorial Chapel.

Through dramatic and often daring growth, what was once a dream of accessible and affordable higher education has evolved into a complex, modern university. IIT's curriculum and its groundbreaking architecture are inseparable and interdependent. Just as Mies's architecture curriculum once shaped his twentieth-century campus master plan, the twenty-first-century campus continues to adapt and grow along with the university.

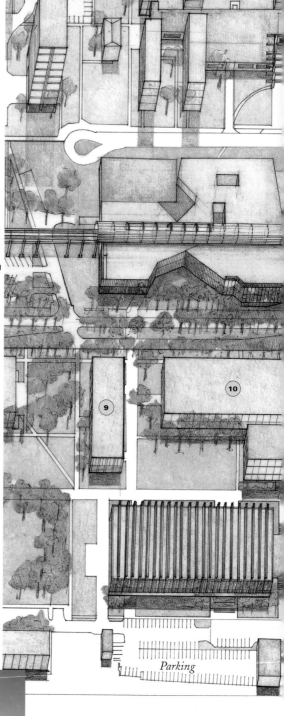

1 | Main Building
2 | Machinery Hall
3 | Minerals and Metals Research Building
4 | Cogeneration Facility
5 | Boiler Plant
6 | Engineering Research Building
7 | Armour Mission
8 | Armour Flats
9 | Alumni Memorial Hall
10 | Metallurgical and Chemical Engineering Building (Perlstein Hall)

Parking

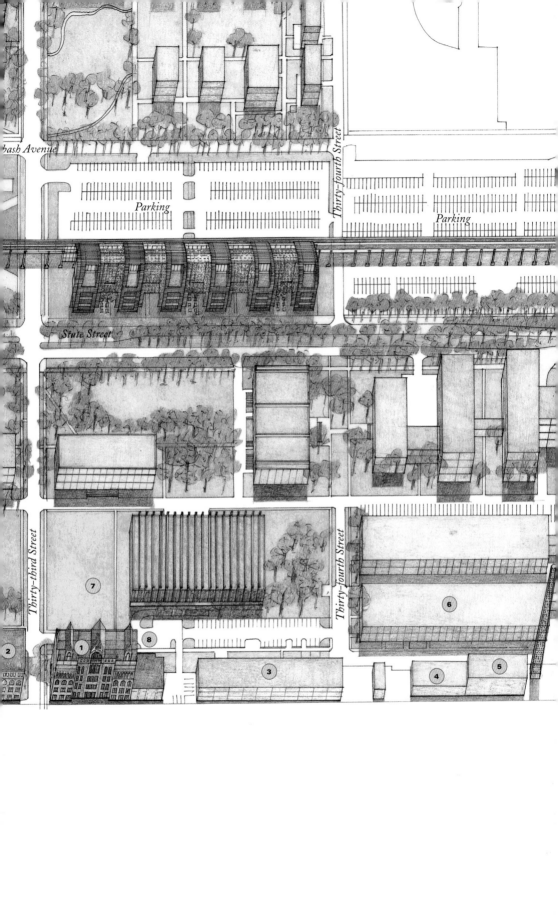

Main Building

1. Main Building   *Patton & Fisher, 1891–93*

The best place to begin a walking tour is with IIT's oldest standing structure, now officially a Chicago landmark. There the difference between the traditionalism embraced by the nineteenth century and the modernism later employed by Mies is impossible to miss. Architects of the late nineteenth century commonly looked to historical styles for inspiration, and the Romanesque, identified by round arches and heavily rusticated masonry walls, provided the sober monumentality that the Armour Institute (the school's original name) desired for its first academic building. As realized here, the lowest floor and the addition to the south depend upon battered, undressed sandstone walls. The surface of the higher elevation is red pressed brick. One concession to latter-day usage is added ornamentation in terra cotta—notably in columns, capitals, and sills.

Main Building was originally a classroom structure that also contained the library and the school gymnasium. Built at a cost of $500,000, it was dedicated to Philip Danforth Armour, Jr., son of the school's founder, Philip Armour. Today it serves as an administration building.

The most arresting interior feature is a group of three adjoining stained-glass windows that overlooks the landing of the main staircase. Measuring seventeen by eighteen feet and composed of more than a million pieces of Tiffany glass, it was designed by Edwin P. Sperry, head artist of the Church Glass and Decorating Company of New York and an associate of Louis Comfort Tiffany. Five full-length figures enact a symbolic narrative characteristic of late nineteenth-century institutional monuments. In the center panel, a classically attired male representing Success is shown taking a crown of triumph from the altar of fame, which is inscribed *famam factis extendit* ("he extends his fame by his deeds"). The female figures in the flanking windows symbolize Heat, Motion, Gravity, and Light, names appropriate to a technological school. The enclosing frame of Carrara marble, the work of John W. Foster of Armour &Co., resembles the facade of a Roman temple, replete with an entablature and four Corinthian columns resting on a podium. Other interior appointments deserving of attention include the bronze wainscoting on the columns in the registrar's office on the main floor (originally the library) and the decorative cast-iron handrails of the main staircase.

Main Building was more than a half-century old when, during the winter of 1947–48, the attic tower was damaged by fire and taken down. Several decades later, in 1982, the institute substantially renovated the building. In the registrar's office, a mezzanine and a number of partitions were removed, and in the process four theretofore concealed stained-glass windows—gifts respectively of the classes of 1897, 1898, 1899, and 1900—were uncovered and restored. Work on the exterior included the cleaning and tuckpointing of masonry and the replacement of old wood-framed windows with new glass, set in anodized aluminum frames.

Stained-glass windows by Edwin P. Sperry

LEFT: *Plaque by Frederick Hibbard*
RIGHT: *Plaque by George E. Ganiere*

The corridor of the main floor remains largely as it was in its original state. Cracks in its marble floor mark decades-long pedestrian traffic patterns, and a pair of commemorative plaques adorns its walls: one by Chicago sculptor George E. Ganiere memorializing Frank Wakely Gunsaulus, Armour Institute's first president, and the other by Chicago sculptor Frederick Hibbard (class of 1912) and dedicated to Winfield Peck (class of 1912).

2. Machinery Hall   *Patton & Fisher, 1901*

The first Armour Institute building completed in the twentieth century, this recently designated Chicago landmark fulfilled the need for classrooms that Main Building was unable to satisfy as the school grew. Its resemblance to Main in style (Neoromanesque) and materials (red pressed brick with terra cotta trim) is evidence that it was designed by the same architectural firm. Though smaller in size and built on a more modest budget, the building exhibits several attractive features, including an overall simplicity of form and a uniquely corbelled brick cornice that turns the corner neatly and elegantly.

The original function of Machinery Hall has been taken over by later IIT buildings. Today it serves chiefly as a depot for storage and, from time to time, a temporary locale for operations awaiting permanent homes elsewhere on campus. A maintenance garage at 3240 South Federal, just north of Machinery Hall, was also designed in 1901 by Patton & Fisher. It is a small, unimposing structure built of brick, but some of its ornamentation, like the egg-and-dart frieze and sculptural keystones over the windows, leave a positive impression. To the original inscription of "Armour Laboratories" the words "Institute of Technology" were appended, well after the building was constructed.

Machinery Hall

3. IIT Research Institute (IITRI) Minerals and Metals Research Building *Ludwig Mies van der Rohe, 1943*

IITRI Addition *Ludwig Mies van der Rohe, 1958*

The Minerals and Metals Research Building is the first structure on campus by Mies van der Rohe. His earliest completed work in the United States, the building exploits the advantages of steel, a material more typical of construction in the U.S. than in Germany. Well-suited to the technological needs of the day in general, steel also seemed an appropriate choice for a technical university in particular. Mies constructed the entire frame of the Minerals and Metals Research Building, vertical and horizontal members alike, of wide-flange beams and mullions. Freestanding walls of the building were designed in glass and brick and were inserted within the frame. Indicative of the primacy of structure in the abstract, the wide-flange steel section would later become Mies's signature element.

That the building occupied a transitional place in Mies's body of work is apparent on the south end elevation, where columns and spandrels are connected by bolts rather than by welding, which later became standard at IIT. Nonetheless, the closest thing to its dynamic use of steel in the U.S. was the industrial plant architecture of Albert Kahn. Relative to the vocabulary of buildings at other American technical universities, the Minerals and Metals Research Building qualified as a revolutionary structural effort.

TOP: *Minerals and Metals Research Building, 1944*
© *Chicago Historical Society, HB-07890–A, photographer Hedrich Blessing*
OPPOSITE: *Minerals and Metals Research Building, 1958 addition*

Oddly enough, the columns of the building are not visible at all on the exterior, where a glass wall and a brick apron conceal them. Early sketches suggest that at one point Mies did consider revealing the columns externally but ruled against it, a decision that resulted, unhappily, in cracks in the brick wall at the mullion points. In later IIT buildings, he exposed the columns on the face of the wall, between brick spandrel panels laid in Flemish bond.

On the building's interior, the wide-flange of the fully constituted frame is most evident. The differentiation of the interior, which houses a three-story foundry hall flanked by three floors of laboratories and offices, was made readable originally on the end wall of the building. There the surface of the metal frame appeared on the brick walls as a geometric pattern. Also externally indicated, by the wider fascia at the second-story level, was the balcony that overlooks the main floor of the hall. This early display of Mies's oft-quoted concern for clarity of expression led some observers to speculate that the building's structural system was derived from the geometric abstractions of the Dutch modernist painter Piet Mondrian, an influence that Mies denied. The truth behind this speculation became academic when the wall was made part of the interior by the 1958 six-bay addition to the north, which maintained the height and width of the first structure but did not continue the space of the foundry hall. Thus, with no need to suggest the presence of a large space, Mies was content to extend the pattern of clerestory windows around the three added elevations, rendered in brick laid in English bond.

It is worth adding that the Minerals and Metals Research Building—a relatively long, narrow, single-span structure—figured in a typological distinction made by Mies. He saw such buildings as "Gothic," since they were linear systems that could be cut off anywhere along their length. Double-span structures with square bays were regarded as characteristic of the Renaissance, hence "Classical."

IIT Cogeneration Facility (right) with Boiler Plant (left)

4. IIT Cogeneration Facility   *Ludwig Mies van der Rohe, 1946*

Standing directly south of the Minerals and Metals Research Building is the Cogeneration Facility, central to the use of electricity, heating, and cooling on campus. Although built just three years after its glass-and-steel neighbor, its brick wall-bearing construction is more characteristic of Mies's later work at IIT.

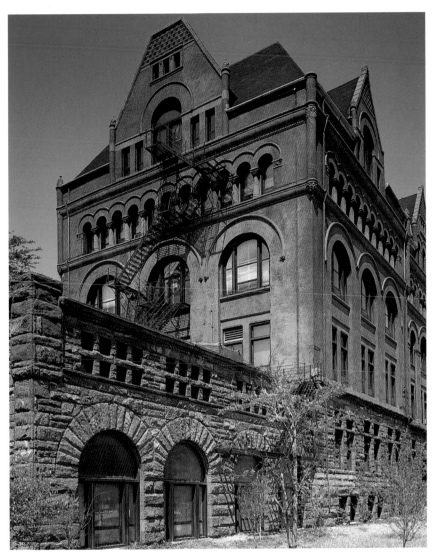

Original IIT Boiler Plant

5. IIT Boiler Plant   *Ludwig Mies van der Rohe, 1946*

The central heating plant of Armour Institute of Technology was once located at the south end of Main Building, and the base of the old stack is still visible. But with the number of buildings promised by Mies's master plan, a new facility was needed. Construction of the new boiler plant began in 1945 and was completed in the following year. The compact rectangular building has five bays on the east and west elevations and three on the north and south. The simple shell housed the boiler and coal hopper (later replaced by gas), with an operating platform at the second-floor level. The Boiler Plant provides a striking example of Mies's regard for simplicity of expression and elegant proportion, even within structures built for strictly industrial functions.

IITRI Engineering Research Building

The bays of all four elevations were defined by columns and mullions but with varying fenestrations. The elevation most readily visible to pedestrians is on the east and features strip windows between in-wall columns at the first- and second-floor levels and just below the fascia level.

In 1964 six bays were added to the northern end of Mies's building by architects Sargent & Lundy. A more recent addition is the Cogeneration Facility, completed in 1990 farther to the north after plans by another firm, National Energy Systems of Lombard, Illinois, a subsidiary of the Marmon Group.

6. IITRI Engineering Research Building

Ludwig Mies van der Rohe, 1944–52

Begun during World War II, when structural steel was difficult to come by, the Engineering Research Building was constructed in reinforced concrete, a material that later became customary in IITRI buildings. The shortage of steel also led to changes in details like window frames, a number of which (still visible on the western elevation) were made of wood. Especially worthy of note is the quality of the brick employed: laid in English bond, it is still in virtually perfect condition after more than half a century. Also

OPPOSITE: *IITRI Engineering Research Building*

exceptional, at the northern end of the building, is the lucid reveal between the brick and the poured-in-place concrete.

Measuring four by six bays, the Engineering Research Building contains two floors and a partial mezzanine. Prior to the construction of the John Crerar/Kemper Library (now the Paul V. Galvin Library), the university's main library was housed in the southern section of this building, moved there from the university's Main Building upon its completion.

7. Armour Mission *Burnham & Root, 1886*

This building, erected directly east of the site later occupied by Main

Armour Mission, lintel

Building, may have served as a stylistic model for the latter's Neoromanesque design. Built in 1886 as a home for the Plymouth Mission (later called the Armour Mission), the building was turned into Armour Institute's student union in 1938. Razed in 1962, its one remaining material relic is a lintel with incised, hand-carved letters spelling out the name "Armour Mission," which originally surmounted the main entrance. Today the stone lies on the ground in front of Main Building. The area north of the Mission's site, now occupied by Perlstein and Wishnick halls, was laid out in 1894 as Ogden Field, an athletic field named after Armour board president J. Ogden Armour, who donated $250,000 toward its creation. (This area was nicknamed the Bog because of its muddy condition following rainfall.)

Armour Mission, built in 1886

8. Armour Flats, later including Physics Building and Chapin Hall *Patton & Fisher, 1886*

The Flats, built east of Armour Mission, consisted of 194 suites of apartments, three to four stories high, two to a floor and all with street fronts. Organized around an inner courtyard, the apartments took up a full city block. The basement and first story of the street facades were constructed of Lake Superior variegated sandstone, and the upper floors were faced with red pressed brick. Vaguely Queen Anne in style and notable for the dominant turret at the northeast corner of Thirty-third and Dearborn, the Flats harmonized aesthetically with the Mission. Most of the apartments were demolished in 1918. The northernmost portion, across from the Armour Mission, was converted into Physics Hall and Chapin Hall. These last components of the original group came down in 1967.

Alumni Memorial Hall, 1947
© *Chicago Historical Society, HB-9767-A, photographer Hedrich Blessing*

Alumni Memorial Hall, 1946
© *Chicago Historical Society, HB-09233-C, photographer Hedrich Blessing*

9. **Alumni Memorial Hall** *Ludwig Mies van der Rohe, 1945–46*

The singular importance of Alumni Memorial Hall derives from its crucial place in the chronology of Mies's IIT buildings. It was here that he effectively brought to completion the vocabulary of form he had only begun to express in the Minerals and Metals Research Building. In the latter work, the wide flange was introduced, but in a sense still tentatively, more visible on the interior than on the exterior, with the connections of beams and columns made by bolts rather than by the welding process used in later buildings. In Alumni Memorial Hall a distinction is made, with uniquely perceptible clarity, between the primary steel-skeleton structure and the secondary structure of the exterior wall. The former consists of wide-flange columns encased in fireproofing concrete and covered with steel plates; the latter, of I-beams welded to the steel plates. Each of these components and their connections are expressively exposed at the corners, while a recessed channel between I-beam and brick infill avoided a possible untrue adjacency between the edges of two materials. Moreover, the curtain mullions run regularly along the elevation at intervals of twelve feet. That dimension was determined by the module governing the campus layout and kept short enough to prevent the brick infill from cracking, as it had in the Minerals and Metals Research Building.

Perlstein Hall

Because commercially available sections in either steel or aluminum were not affordable in the years immediately following World War II, custom-made steel sections were used in the building's hopper windows. Originally designed for the U.S. Navy, Alumni Hall contained a two-story space used as an armory. After the war a portion of the building was taken over by the School of Architecture (which would move into its own quarters in S. R. Crown Hall in 1956). In 1972 a floor was installed within the two-story space, and offices were reorganized to accommodate several other IIT departments. Still worthy of attention on the interior is the quality of the white oak millwork and the equally engaging simplicity with which it is crafted.

10. IIT Metallurgical and Chemical Engineering Building (Perlstein Hall) *Ludwig Mies van der Rohe, 1944–46*

In many respects the form of this building, like that of a number of others on the campus, follows the precedent of Alumni Memorial Hall. Nonetheless, some of the most important elements of the vocabulary mastered in Alumni evolved over the course of work on Perlstein Hall. This is evident in the hundreds of drawings by Mies and his associates, in which such problems related to the distinction between primary and secondary

Perlstein Hall

structure, one- and two-way span structures, the expression of steel within the limitations of fireproofing, and the treatment of multiple elevations within a single building were confronted.

Perlstein Hall is sited closest to the corner of State and Thirty-third streets, the intersection that effectively forms the gateway to the campus. The lawn directly in front of it accommodates a single-jet fountain, designed by the late IIT professor Myron Goldsmith and notable for its radial reductivist symmetry. The building itself is bilaterally symmetrical. The major feature of the ground floor's south end is a wedge-shaped auditorium, the doors of which are made of the white oak made commonplace in Mies's campus buildings. Immediately to the north of that space, stairs lead to the basement and the upper floor. Beyond the stairs is an open courtyard. Classrooms on the east and west ends empty into a pair of corridors that provide access to the two-story operations laboratory at the north end of the building.

The laboratory was meant to house an overhead crane too large to fit into a space true to the standard twelve-foot campus module. A width of thirty-six feet prompted Mies to clad the laboratory in a two-story brick wall erected outside the columns. Somewhat reminiscent of the foundry hall located in the Minerals and Metals Research Building, this one-way-span space gave Mies the opportunity to pursue the concept of the clear span, which would be fully expressed in later buildings such as Crown Hall.

Perlstein Hall, lobby, with Barcelona chairs by Mies van der Rohe

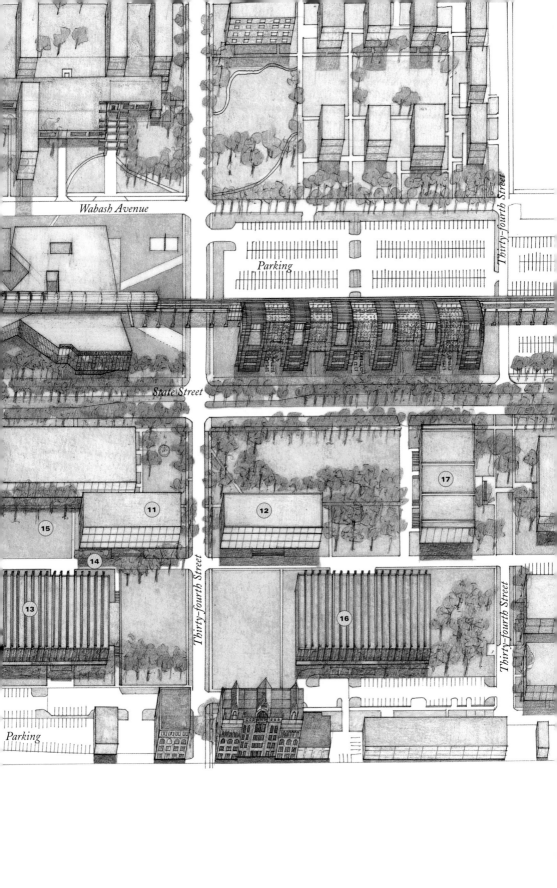

Wabash Avenue

Parking

Thirty-fourth Street

State Street

⑮

⑪

⑭

⑬

Parking

⑫

⑰

⑯

Thirty-fourth Street

11. IIT Chemistry Building (Wishnick Hall)

Ludwig Mies van der Rohe, 1945–46

With the completion of Wishnick Hall, the stylistic consistency of Mies's IIT classroom buildings was clearly established. Its exterior relates it visibly to Alumni Memorial and Perlstein halls, differing from them most obviously in Wishnick's rise to three (rather than two) stories. There are other distinctions—minor ones—readable in plan rather than in primary or secondary structure. The foyer of Wishnick Hall is located on the long side (rather than the short end) of the building. Like the auditorium it leads to, it occupies the central three of nine bays. As at Perlstein Hall, the foyer side of the auditorium boasts a single, gently curved surface of white oak millwork.

Wishnick Hall's height recalls the second phase of Mies's master plan, in which he decided to reverse the order of the heights of the buildings flanking the campus entry at Thirty-third and State streets. His intent was to ensure that those buildings with three stories would be sited behind those with two, thus allowing both types to be seen more readily at a distance.

12. IIT Electrical Engineering and Physics Building (Siegel Hall) *Ludwig Mies van der Rohe, 1954–55*

Virtually identical to Wishnick Hall in plan and elevation, Siegel Hall differs only in function. Its three-story height, together with its location directly across Thirty-third Street from its twin, also recalls the second phase of Mies's master plan (see discussion of Wishnick Hall above).

Siegel Hall occupies a site originally meant for the Lewis Building, which would have accommodated the activities of Lewis Institute, the Chicago arts and humanities college that merged with Armour Institute of Technology in 1940 to form Illinois Institute of Technology. Mies undertook the design of the Lewis Building, but the university's priorities prevented its construction. The administrative offices of the Lewis College of Sciences and Letters eventually took over space in the Life Sciences Research Building, built in 1966 by Skidmore, Owings & Merrill (see p. 67).The Lewis Building was not the only structure that failed to materialize in the area flanking Thirty-third Street that came to be known as Mies Alley. A Mechanical Engineering Building planned for south of Perlstein Hall was never realized, chiefly due to insufficient funds. Had it been built, it would have completed a substantial portion of the symmetrical pattern envisioned by Mies in his second master plan.

TOP: *Wishnick Hall*
BOTTOM: *Siegel Hall*

Grover M. Hermann Hall

13. Grover M. Hermann Hall   *Skidmore Owings & Merrill, 1961*

From the standpoint of Mies's admirers, Hermann Hall has several counts against it. It was designed by another architect (Walter Netsch, of the Chicago office of Skidmore, Owings & Merrill), following IIT's decision to withdraw all campus commissions from Mies. Moreover, it took the place of the student union that had figured centrally in Mies's original master plan, before it was abandoned in 1952 along with the Library and Administration Building. And while it clearly follows Mies stylistically, it does so, Mies's supporters say, ineptly. That opinion has, in fact, been shared by a majority of competent observers over the years. The late Carl W. Condit, one of America's most honored architectural historians, branded Hermann Hall "an inferior version of Crown Hall."

The association is obvious from the first look, and the judgment from the second. The girders that ride above the roof are clearly based on the plate girders atop Crown Hall, but those at Hermann Hall are supported by indented columns visible only on the interior. Thus the facade is a curtain wall divided solely by slender mullions. The logical relationship of girder, columns, and mullions evident at Crown Hall is absent here.

Nonetheless, Hermann Hall, known also as the Hermann Union Building, has served IIT for more than forty years. It is a three-story structure, its largest area given over to a 900-seat auditorium located

The Rock

midway between the north and south ends of the building. Since the services of some of the former spaces, most notably a large cafeteria, have been taken over by The McCormick Tribune Campus Center and the adjacent renovated Commons Building (see pages 55–57), Hermann Hall has become a multipurpose conference center. The auditorium as well as a lounge on the east side and a ballroom to the south continue to function as they have in the past. Nearly all the other areas have been turned into meeting rooms answering a variety of needs.

14. The Rock

One of the typically collegiate traditions at IIT involves a two-to-four-ton stone that rests mostly submerged in the ground just south of the walkway leading to Hermann Hall. It attracts attention mostly because of its lively painted surface. Colors, images, and messages have been applied to it regularly over the years, usually by students with some special cause in mind. (Following the September 11, 2001 terrorist attacks, the Rock displayed an image of the American flag.)

The Rock was given to Armour Institute in 1893 by the Canadian Copper Company of Sudsbury, Ontario, which had included it in one of the exhibits at the World's Columbian Exposition on Chicago's South Side.

Man on a Bench by George Segal

Once in the possession of the institute, it was placed near the entrance to the Armour Mission building and transferred to its present location when Hermann Hall was completed in 1962. Its value derives less from its mineral content—mostly nickel, with a few ounces of gold—than from the fondness the school's community has grown to feel for it.

Accordingly, the Rock has its history of pranks—most notably, the attempt by students one night in 1969 to dig it free and move it to another spot on campus. By morning they were forced to abandon their efforts, but they had managed to remove enough earth to lower the Rock considerably. And there it remains. Legend has it that one of the students' shovels is forever entombed beneath it.

15. *Man on a Bench* *sculpture by George Segal, 1986*

George Segal made a major name for himself during the 1960s, when pop art dominated the international art scene. His association with the movement derives from his habit of placing his sculpted figures on or next to objects lifted from actual vernacular environments. In this instance the figure of an adult male taken from a living model, cast in bronze, and sealed with white acrylic resin, is seated on a green park bench appropriated, rather than fabricated, by the artist.

Man on a Bench, located immediately west of Perlstein Hall and north of Wishnick Hall, was the first piece of public sculpture displayed outdoors on the IIT campus. Commissioned as part of the university's observance of the centennial of Mies van der Rohe's birth, it was made possible by a grant from the B. F. Ferguson Monument Fund of the Art Institute of Chicago, with additional funding from Daniel J. Terra, founder of the Terra Museum of American Art, and Victor J. Axelrod, president of the Banner Construction Company.

The figure clearly bears African-American features and appears to be surveying the meadow enclosed by Perlstein, Wishnick, and Hermann halls. Although most interpretations have stressed the sculpture's meditative mood, Segal recalled his own motives in greater detail: "After my trip to Chicago, I found myself thinking of several things: the calm order of the campus, the memory of Mies, and the concerned sensitivity of the school to the surrounding community."

Paul V. Galvin Library

16. Paul V. Galvin Library *Skidmore, Owings & Merrill, 1962*

The architect responsible for Hermann Hall also produced Galvin Library, and the kinship of their design and structural system is clear from most of their exterior elements. The main difference is that the entrance to Galvin Hall was placed a full level below grade, accessible by a staircase to the north and a ramp to the south.

Sited directly across Thirty-third Street from Hermann Hall, the library was originally built as a new home for the John Crerar Library, a private research facility named after the Chicago industrialist and established in 1894. Strong in science, technology, and medicine, the Crerar Library had been housed in the Marshall Field Department Store in downtown Chicago until 1920, when it took over its own space in a newly constructed office building at 86 East Randolph Street. Financial difficulties later led to its merger with the IIT Library. The Skidmore building served as a repository of the Crerar holdings and of the rare book collection of Chicago insurance magnate James S. Kemper. When the Crerar Library was transferred to the University of Chicago in 1985, the building was renamed the Paul V. Galvin Library, in honor of the founder of the Motorola Company.

The lowest level of the Galvin Library now provides space for special collections (including the James S. Kemper Collection), current journals, the Academic Research Center, Library Technical Services, the University Archives, and Access Services. The upper level contains stacks and study carrels.

TOP: *Crown Hall, construction*
BOTTOM: *Mies van der Rohe with students in Crown Hall*

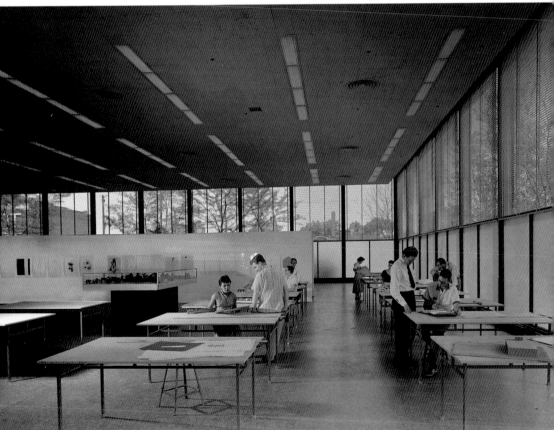

TOP: *Crown Hall, aerial view, 1955–56*
© *Chicago Historical Society, HB-18506-R3, photographer Hedrich Blessing*
BOTTOM: *Crown Hall, interior, 1955–56*
© *Chicago Historical Society, HB-18506-F4, photographer William Engdahl*

17. Architecture and Institute of Design Building, known as S. R. Crown Hall *Ludwig Mies van der Rohe, 1956*

By consensus the most architecturally significant building on the IIT campus, and designated a Chicago landmark, S. R. Crown Hall was designed to accommodate the school's departments of architecture, design, and planning. Prior to its completion, Mies had been on the faculty for nearly two decades, conducting his classes in settings not originally meant for architectural education. Thus the prospect of a building designed specifically for the pursuit of his own discipline was especially close to his heart.

The singular importance of the finished work, to which he devoted six years, derives from a number of factors but principally from his first material realization of a large-scale clear-span structure. Column-free, the building fulfilled another of Mies's major objectives: the creation of universal space. The rationale of the latter concept was well expressed by Peter Carter, who wrote in his 1972 study, *Mies van der Rohe at Work*, "Mies van der Rohe discovered that one or more related activities may be brought together and unified within a single space, a possibility which has the advantage of a built-in provision for change, precisely because the structural shell is independent of the functional subdivisions."

Mies had produced several designs that accomplished this end prior to Crown Hall, but none had been built. He had also completed one clear-span structure—the Farnsworth House of 1951—but this private residence is modest in size. The dimensions of Crown Hall—120 by 220 by 18 feet high—are monumental by contrast. The structural system consists primarily of four welded-steel portal frames, each made of a pair of columns carrying a six-foot-deep plate girder. The roof is hung from these frames, which are spaced sixty feet on center. The exterior walls are wholly of glass set between steel mullions that have been welded to the floor and roof fasciae. The facade module is composed of an upper light of clear glass and two lower lights of sandblasted glass. Beneath the latter are louvers providing air intake. The symmetrically composed interior is a single space subdivided only by two nonstructural service shafts, a pair of stairs leading to a basement, and areas meant for administration and the exhibition of work. The main entrance is on the south, accessible via a staircase leading to a deck and another stair, then to the doors. Here Mies followed the precedent of the Farnsworth House, where the stair supports, concealed beneath the travertine stretchers, create a floating effect.

Although the building led to other examples of universal space in clear-span structure, Mies's motive here bore directly on his view of architectural education. The idea of students and teachers of all levels of experience assembling and working within sight of each other greatly appealed to him, since it reminded him of the *Bauhütte*, the medieval shelter in which designers, craftsmen, and laborers worked side by side.

Crown Hall, interior views

Crown Hall, night view

In the course of designing Crown Hall, Mies experimented with a variety of forms. Drawings most likely done early in the process show a building akin to others on the campus, with a columnar grid and walls of brick infill set below rows of windows. Once the clear-span idea became fixed in his mind, he considered supporting the roof by deep open trusses—five and sometimes even six in number—before finally deciding on four plate girders. That his intentions were unconventional by standards of the day is evident from the fact that IIT, in order to obtain a building permit, was obliged to identify Crown Hall as a warehouse rather than an academic building. Only then did the city place its stamp of approval on plans for a structure whose interior was not subdivided into classrooms.

The lower level of the building originally housed the Institute of Design (ID), a school begun elsewhere in Chicago in the 1930s by a multi-talented Hungarian refugee, László Moholy-Nagy, who, like Mies, had been on the faculty of Germany's famed Bauhaus. The ID was taken over by IIT in 1949 and room was made for it in Crown Hall. In 1993 the institute moved to its own quarters closer to Chicago's Loop, and the space it formerly occupied in Crown Hall was turned into studios, offices, and an architectural library. Changes in the area around Crown Hall are also worth noting. At the time the building opened, Thirty-fourth Street crossed the campus. Thus the entrance to Crown Hall was placed on its south facade, facing the street. To the south was the Institute of Gas Technology Complex. Although the street has been covered over with lawns and pathways, the entrance remains as designed by Mies. Plans for the restoration of Crown Hall are being conducted by a committee of architects and preservationists, including most notably the Chicago firm of Krueck & Sexton as well as Gunny Harboe of McClier Corporation of Chicago.

Crown Hall

Robert F. Carr Memorial Chapel

18. Robert F. Carr Memorial Chapel of Saint Savior

Ludwig Mies van der Rohe, 1952

The nonsectarian Carr Memorial Chapel is the only ecclesiastical work ever constructed to Mies's design. The building went through two major planning stages. The first scheme consisted of two parts: the chapel proper, conceived as a steel-framed structure with a basement, and a nearby parish house with living quarters for a chaplain and a parish hall with a conference room and foyer.

As completed, the chapel is more modest, both in planning and scale. It is a single, one-story building measuring thirty-seven by sixty feet. Its end elevations are identical, although the glass on the east entry side is clear while that on the west is sandblasted opaque. Support is provided by a brick bearing wall, which, like the steel-frame roof, is fully visible from within. The plan is basilican, with two side aisles and a center aisle leading to the sanctuary. In this instance Mies's inclination toward refined materials employed with utmost simplicity is especially evident. The altar is a solid block of Roman travertine resting upon a platform of the same substance. The curtain behind the altar is of natural shantung silk. Slender lineaments of highly polished stainless steel form the cross and altar rail. At the rear of

Chapel, interior

the chapel, accessible through doorways lined with white oak, are the sacristy, choir, and restrooms.

19. Commons Building   *Ludwig Mies van der Rohe, 1953*

At the time the Commons was completed, it contained a dining area with adjacent kitchen, grocery store, snack shop, valet shop, post office, bookstore, and doctors' suite. The basement housed a bowling alley and recreation and meeting rooms. The Commons now serves as the main campus dining facility, with most of the previous functions taken over by The McCormick Tribune Campus Center upon its opening in 2003.

Both buildings were designed to serve student and faculty social activities rather than for academic purposes, and accordingly both are located close to the campus's housing and fraternity complex. The connection of the center and the Commons has not deprived the latter of its original character. Its exposed steel structure with glass and brick infill panels, treated in the simplest fashion, elegantly exemplifies what Mies meant by his own frequently expressed goal of *beinahe nichts* ("almost nothing").

TOP: *Commons Building, 1954 © Chicago Historical Society, HB-17346–C, photographer Hedrich Blessing*
BOTTOM: *Commons Building, 1954 © Chicago Historical Society, HB-17346–F, photographer William Engdahl*

TOP: *Commons Building*
BOTTOM: *Commons Building, interiors*

Because the Commons is a single story above grade, it is free of the fireproofing required for buildings of more than one level. A roof structure of beams and girders is supported by wide-flange steel columns with precast-concrete ceiling slabs resting on them. The system is fully visible in the sixteen-foot-high interior.

Association of American Railroads Complex

20. Association of American Railroads (AAR)
Complex *Ludwig Mies van der Rohe*

AAR Technical Center, 1950

AAR Mechanical Engineering Research Laboratory, 1953

AAR Engineering Research Laboratory, 1956

Both the Technical Center and the Engineering Research Laboratory are based fundamentally on the model of a steel system with glass and brick curtain walls set by Alumni Memorial Hall and followed in Perlstein, Wishnick, and Siegel halls. Unlike those four buildings, however, the corner detail of the Technical Center is notable for brick that rises higher at the base of the wall before the steel begins above. In a more noticeable contrast, the corner of the Engineering Research Laboratory features back-to-back wide-flanges that run the entire length of the column. A similar use of the wide-flange is evident in the Mechanical Engineering Research Laboratory, but there the treatment of the elevation of the building is unique among Mies's campus designs, since brick is used on most of the two short side, while the fenestration on the long sides consists of bays, each with twelve windows. Today the Technical Center accommodates the VanderCook College of Music. The two laboratory buildings have been leased by the Chicago Transit Authority, which uses them for instruction of trainees in safety measures and repair of transit vehicles.

OPPOSITE TOP: *Association of American Railroads Complex, 1958*
© *Chicago Historical Society, HB-21089-B, photographer Hedrich Blessing*
OPPOSITE BOTTOM: *Association of American Railroads Complex, interior, 1954*
© *Chicago Historical Society, HB-17346-A, photographer Hedrich Blessing (image cropped)*

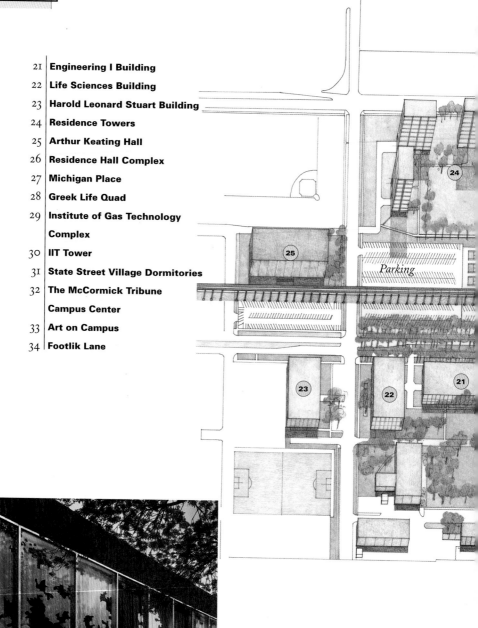

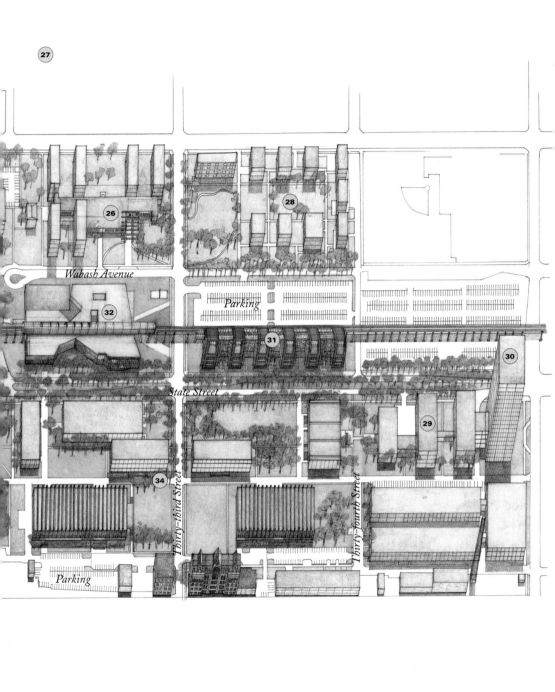

27

26

Wabash Avenue

28

32

Parking

31

30

State Street

29

34

Thirty-third Street

Thirty-fourth Street

Parking

Engineering I Building, rendering

21. Engineering I Building   *Skidmore, Owings & Merrill, 1968*

Myron Goldsmith, a student and later employee of Mies van der Rohe, served as the lead architect of the Engineering I, the Life Sciences, and the Harold Leonard Stuart buildings. The obvious resemblance between these and most of the earlier academic buildings at IIT may be accounted for by Goldsmith's recollection that in all three instances he found Mies's structural and spatial vocabulary fully successful, calling for no substantial deviation. The viewer may observe that Mies's windows above the brick infill in such works as Alumni, Perstein, Wishnick, and Siegel halls are subdivided while Goldsmith's are not. Otherwise the similarity between the efforts of teacher and student is obvious. The Engineering I Building is two stories in height.

OPPOSITE: *Path leading to Engineering I Building*

Harold Leonard Stuart Building

22. Life Sciences Building *Skidmore, Owings & Merrill, 1966*

The Life Sciences Building, which is is connected to the Engineering I Building by an underground passage, is virtually identical with it in plan and elevation. It occupies the former site of the Plymouth Congregational Church, which figured in the "prehistory" of IIT (see page 1 of the Introduction).

23. Harold Leonard Stuart Building
Skidmore, Owings & Merrill, 1971

This building, which houses the Office of Technology Services, Computer Science, and ROTC, is named for the IIT alumnus whose bequest of $5 million made its construction possible.

OPPOSITE: *Life Sciences Building*

TOP: *Residence Hall (unspecified), interior, 1953* © *Chicago Historical Society, HB-16736-C, photographer Hedrich Blessing*
BOTTOM: *Carman Hall, 1953* © *Chicago Historical Society, HB-29057-D/F, photographer Hedrich Blessing*

Residence Towers, aerial view, 1955
© *Chicago Historical Society, HB–18783–A, photographer Hedrich Blessing*

24. Residence Towers

Bailey Hall Apartments *Ludwig Mies van der Rohe, 1955*

Cunningham Hall Apartments *Ludwig Mies van der Rohe, 1955*

Gunsaulus Hall Apartments *Skidmore, Owings & Merrill, 1950*

Carman Hall Apartments *Ludwig Mies van der Rohe, 1953*

Following the close of World War II, IIT's enrollment increased, creating a need for new residential space for staff, faculty, and married students. This led to the construction of these four apartment towers. The buildings began to appear in the early 1950s on a site at the northeast corner of the campus. While Mies van der Rohe was the logical choice as designer, he was occupied at the time with several other projects in Chicago, including Crown Hall and 860–880 North Lake Shore Drive. Thus the commission for the first building, named for Frank Gunsaulus (see following page), went to the office of Skidmore, Owings & Merrill, which produced a building generically related to the modernist style already introduced at IIT by Mies.

The three towers that followed the construction of Gunsaulus Hall are recognizably by Mies. Built in reinforced concrete, they rely on a structural system that recalls his treatment of the Promontory Apartment Building completed in 1949 on South Lake Shore Drive. In that building the three-unit windows run above brick panels indented slightly behind the supporting columns, which increase in thickness nearer to the ground, where the weight and overturning forces are greatest. Except for their four-unit windows, the IIT buildings are true to the Promontory model. Equally

Carman Hall, 1953 © *Chicago Historical Society, HB-16736-B, photographer Hedrich Blessing*

typical, and reminiscent of the 860–880 North Lake Shore Drive apartment buildings, was Mies's decision to set the fully glazed ground-floor lobby back from the facade and to align the columnar grids of all three buildings on the site.

The names given to the four towers recall figures of stature in the administrative history of Armour Institute of Technology and Lewis Institute, the two schools that joined in 1940 to form IIT. George Noble Carman was the first director of Lewis Institute, and Frank Wakely Gunsaulus was the first president of Armour Institute. Alex D. Bailey was the board chairman of Lewis, and James D. Cunningham, of Armour Institute at the time of the two institutions' merger. Cunningham became the first board chairman of IIT.

TOP: *Bailey Hall*
BOTTOM: *Gunsaulus Hall*

TOP: *Arthur Keating Hall, drawing*
BOTTOM: *Arthur Keating Hall*

One of five IIT campus buildings designed by Myron Goldsmith of Skidmore, Owings & Merrill, Keating Hall differs from the other four most obviously in that it does not closely resemble any of Mies van der Rohe's work at IIT. The difference may be accounted for by its function, which is that of a sports center.

That basic dissimilarity aside, in some respects the building is recognizably related to the rest of the campus. Goldsmith gave it the form of a clear-span structure, with plate girders supporting the roof from its underside. The exterior is clad in a curtain wall of multicolored glass. A column-free main floor, large enough to accommodate a wide range of indoor sports, features a gymnasium with seating for two thousand spectators. At the south end of the ground floor is the Olympic-size Ekco swimming pool; at the north end are practice and exercise rooms as well as handball and racquet ball courts. Keating Hall replaced a gymnasium that had earlier stood on Thirty-second Street between Dearborn and State streets. To the east of the building is a baseball field.

26. Residence Hall Complex

Farr Hall *Skidmore, Owings & Merrill, 1948*

Fowler Hall *Skidmore, Owings & Merrill, 1948*

North Hall *Mittelbusher & Tourtelot, 1959*

South Hall *Mittelbusher & Tourtelot, 1959*

East Hall *Mittelbusher & Tourtelot, 1963*

Graduate Hall *Mittelbusher & Tourtelot, 1966*

Lewis Hall *Mittelbusher & Tourtelot, 1958, additions 1966*

McCormick Lounge and Dining Hall *Mittelbusher & Tourtelot, 1959*

South Dining Hall *Mittelbusher & Tourtelot, 1959*

The Residence Hall Complex is now known as the McCormick Student Village. Like the Fraternity Complex, it dates from the late 1950s, when enrollment at IIT experienced a significant rise, leading to an increase in the number of faculty and the need for more residential facilities on campus.

Fowler Hall and Farr Hall, both facing Michigan Avenue and a block apart (with Farr adjacent to Thirty-third Street), were designed by Skidmore, Owings & Merrill and constructed as early as 1948. They were followed by

McCormick Student Village
Residence Halls

Illinois Institute of Technology

LEFT: *Farr Hall*
RIGHT: *Fowler Hall*

six buildings, all by Mittelbusher & Tourtelot. The earliest of the latter group, Lewis Hall, directly across Thirty-third Street from Farr Hall, went up in 1958. In the following year North Hall, South Hall, and the McCormick Lounge and Dining Hall were added, the last of these connecting with all the other buildings of the Village and therewith creating an identifiable structural unity. East Hall dates from 1963 and Graduate Hall from 1966, the same year additions were built to Lewis Hall. Farr Hall, which now contains the university's public safety offices, counseling center, and health services, is six bays long, and Fowler Hall is eight bays long. Both buildings are four stories high, with flat roofs. Those attributes are shared by the Mittelbusher & Tourtelot halls, although they are notable for facades with strip windows.

The Residence Hall Complex is executed in a generic modernist style, and like all the rest of the buildings on campus, it follows Mies van der Rohe's lead in the use of buff-colored brick.

OPPOSITE: *McCormick Student Village*

Michigan Place

27. Michigan Place   *David Hovey, 2004*

Michigan Place is a residential community consisting of two buildings located between Michigan Avenue and Indiana Avenue slightly south of Thirty-first Street. Both were designed by David Hovey, an IIT alumnus and a member of the architecture faculty, in a manner typical of that architect's embrace of late modernist simplicity of form. The roofs are flat, the exterior walls of glass separated by strips of anodized aluminum.

OPPOSITE: *Greek Life Quad*

Alpha Sigma Phi © *Chicago Historical Society, HB–25566, photographer Hedrich Blessing*

Greek Life Quad, rendering

28. Greek Life Quad

Phi Kappa Sigma *Karl M. Schmidt, 1958*

Delta Tau Delta *Alfred J. Mell, 1959*

Triangle *Ekroth, Martorano & Ekroth, 1959*

Alpha Sigma Alpha *Mittelbusher & Tourtelot, 1960*

Pi Kappa Phi *Mittelbusher & Tourtelot, 1960*

Sigma Phi Epsilon *Mittelbusher & Tourtelot, 1960*

Kappa Phi Delta *Mittelbusher & Tourtelot, 1960*

The administration of IIT is on record as affirming the positive role
social Greek organizations play in the academic community. The buildings
providing residences for most of the university's seven fraternities and
four sororities are gathered symmetrically around a quadrangle at the
southeast corner of the campus. Each house is served by a resident
adviser, and meals prepared by professional cooks are available to the
residents.

Like the Residence Hall Complex, the buildings comprising the
Fraternity Complex were designed by a variety of architects, all working in
the generic modernist idiom. Each of the houses has its unique floor plan,
but five display nearly identical three-story elevations, consisting of three
bays east and west, seven north and south. The five are the Law House,
Alpha Sigma Alpha, Alpha Epsilon Pi, Pi Kappa Phi, and Sigma Phi Epsilon

(in this building the east and west windows of the second floor are shorter than those of the aforementioned four). Among the remaining four buildings, designed by four different architects, Phi Kappa Sigma is unique in that the eastern portion of the north elevation is clad in lannon stone.

29. Institute of Gas Technology Complex

North Building *Ludwig Mies van der Rohe, 1950*

South Building *Ludwig Mies van der Rohe, 1955*

Power Plant *Schmidt, Garden & Erikson, 1964*

Central Building *Schmidt, Garden & Erikson, 1965*

Crossover *Schmidt, Garden & Erikson, 1977*

The Institute, established in 1941 to carry out research in gas industry technology, was later lodged in five buildings located on the southwest portion of the campus. Two of these were designed by Mies van der Rohe: the North Building (1950), which is being prepared to provide additional space for the College of Architecture, and the South Building (1955). The three structures occupying the intervening space are credited to Schmidt, Garden & Erikson: from north to south, the Power Plant (1964), the Central Building (1965), and the Crossover (1977). All have been leased by the university to private agencies. Once again, the style of all five buildings is generically modernist.

OPPOSITE: *Institute of Gas Technology, 1948*
© *Chicago Historical Society, HB-11568-I, photographer Hedrich Blessing*

30. IIT Tower *Schmidt, Garden & Erikson, 1964*

At nineteen stories, this tower is the tallest building on the IIT campus. Formerly occupied by the IIT Research Institute, the tower is owned by IIT and leased to government agencies, nonprofits, and for-profit research companies.

31. State Street Village Dormitories *Murphy/Jahn, 2003*

These six dormitories, completed in the summer of 2003, constitute the first major architectural addition to the campus in more than forty years. Designed by architect Helmut Jahn, an alumnus of IIT, they are sited side by side, overlooking State Street to the west, with an encompassing view of the main quadrangle anchored by Crown Hall. Together with The McCormick Tribune Campus Center, they form a new eastern edge to the campus.

The five-story units are conceived as three pairs, each of which consists of two dormitory wings flanking a courtyard planted with birches and lined at the rear by an insulated glass wall that rises to the full height of the building. Entry is gained through the courtyard, which leads to a corridor connecting the wings and to a fully glazed passenger elevator visible from the street. Separating one pair of units from its neighbor is a deeper court-yard with another glass wall. The east elevation, which faces the elevated tracks, is covered with insulated glass and polycarbonate screens, resulting in interiors that are substantially free from the noise created by passing trains.

ABOVE: *State Street Village*
OPPOSITE: *IIT Tower* © *Chicago Historical Society, HB-29057, photographer Hedrich Blessing*

State Street Village

The buildings are constructed of reinforced concrete, with the roof and front elevations dressed in custom corrugated stainless-steel panels and dark gray tinted glass framed in aluminum. The profile is a gentle convex curve that alludes, in Jahn's words, "to the streamlined trains and objects of the Art Moderne." The architect's mastery of steel and glass is perceptible throughout, and in this regard, the dormitories are clearly in the finest Miesian tradition. Jahn was also greatly aided by the expert skill of the German structural engineer Werner Sobek, of Stuttgart, who has successfully collaborated with him on other assignments as well.

The interiors, intended to accommodate 367 undergraduate and graduate students, are made up of sixty-six suites and thirty-two apartments with kitchens. All have access to such common spaces as lounges, laundry facilities, garbage disposal, and computer facilities. The furniture was designed by Jahn. Atop each of the three pairs of units is a deck that offers a compelling view of the campus, the nearby neighborhood, and even the downtown skyline.

Murphy/Jahn was awarded the State Street Village commission following a competition in which the finalists were all from the Chicago area: Lohan, Caprile & Goettsch; Krueck & Sexton Architects; Solomon, Cordwell, Buenz; Booth Hansen; Perkins & Will; Dirk Denison Architects; and STL Architects.

32. The McCormick Tribune Campus Center

Rem Koolhaas and the Office of Metropolitan Architecture, with Holabird & Root, 2003

In 1993 IIT formed a national commission composed of faculty, trustees, and informed outsiders and charged them with assessing the school's entire financial, academic, and physical condition. A campaign to raise $250 million, launched three years later, with an initial $120 million gift from the families of alumni Robert Galvin and Robert Pritzker, eventually proved successful. Among the most immediate architectural consequences of the campaign was a new master plan for a reshaped campus, presented by Chicago architect (and grandson of Mies van der Rohe) Dirk Lohan.

An international competition funded by the Richard H. Driehaus Foundation followed. From the fifty-six architects invited from around the globe, five finalists were selected: Peter Eisenman of New York; Zaha Hadid of London; Helmut Jahn and Werner Sobek of Chicago and Stuttgart; Rem Koolhaas and the Office of Metropolitan Architecture of Rotterdam; and Kazuyo Sejima and Ryue Nishizawa of Tokyo. In 1998 the jury awarded the commission to Koolhaas.

The building bearing the name The McCormick Tribune Campus Center was dedicated in the fall of 2003. It is effectively a student union. Like Helmut Jahn's State Street Village dormitories just south across Thirty-third Street, it is located beneath the elevated train track of one of the branches

The McCormick Tribune Campus Center

The McCormick Tribune Campus Center

The McCormick Tribune Campus Center, Exelon Tube

of Chicago's public transportation system. The noise generated by the trains is considerable, and muffling it was a problem for both Jahn and Koolhaas. By putting up a 530-foot-long, elliptically sectioned concrete tube clad in corrugated stainless steel (its upper arc open to the sky) that wraps around the elevated track, Koolhaas dealt with the problem. This solution, like Jahn's glass wall and screens, has been successful.

The two works have little in common formally. Jahn's dormitories are notable for their symmetry of plan and elevation and the neutrality of palette. Externally and internally, Koolhaas's center is dominated by diagonals, and the principal color of the outer walls is a bright orange. The fascia is maroon striped in black. So as to give the State Street facade sufficient height, the architect canted the roof to accommodate the tube. The resulting southern elevation is V-shaped.

The building serves a wide variety of purposes. The most notable spaces are occupied by a theater, a sports bar, a ballroom, a conference room, and a bookstore. Also included are a radio station, a coffee bar, a faculty-staff dining room, Ping Pong and billiard halls, an internal courtyard, a corridor with computers, a convenience store, a suspended bridge lined with plants, an information station, and a welcome center—the last relating the story of IIT and the surrounding Bronzeville. Wall graphics are based on an abstracted standing figure. This motif, designed by the New York studio 2x4, has been treated to produce images of Mies and some of IIT's founding

The McCormick Tribune Campus Center, tube

fathers. The Commons Building (see pp. 55–57), designed by Mies and completed in 1953, is adjacent to the northeast corner of the center. It now functions as the main campus dining area.

33. Art on Campus

Several sculptures, all in the geometric modernist idiom, can be seen on a tour of the campus. Outside Galvin Library there is a piece made of brushed metal cubes and painted metal curved forms stacked atop a Corten steel base. Its title is *Concurrence*, and the artist is Terry Karpowicz. *Antenna Man*, a work composed of vertical tiers of gleaming metal, by Eric Nordgulen, occupies the lounge of Hermann Hall. The lawn north of Alumni Hall is the site of a construction, *Steel Sculpture*, consisting of metal beams bolted and welded together in horizontal, vertical, and diagonal directions. It was fabricated by a group of the university's civil and architectural engineering students and faculty to demonstrate the ways in which metal parts can be connected. Several yards north of that sculpture and just west of Engineering I is a hollow polyhedron in metal, *S. O. O.* by Lincoln Schatz.

Lincoln Schatz, S.O.O., *with Engineering I Building*

34. Footlik Lane

Footlik Lane is the concrete pedestrian walkway that extends north and south from Thirty-first Street to Thirty-fifth Street, east of Hermann Hall and Galvin Library and west of Wishnick Hall, Siegel Hall, and Crown Hall. South Dearborn Street once ran there, but the City of Chicago accepted IIT's request that it be replaced with the path that is part of Mies van der Rohe's campus master plan. Footlik Lane is named in honor of Irving Footlik (class of 1939) and his wife Sylvia.

Morton Park

The Restoration of the Campus Landscape

The IIT campus landscape has a history of its own, dating back to the earliest days of Armour Institute, but as with so much of the school's building program, Mies van der Rohe's tenure figures heavily in the development of the grounds as they present themselves today. During World War II, Mies struck up a relationship with Chicago landscape architect Alfred Caldwell, in whom he reposed sufficient confidence to invite him to redesign the campus landscape. He also appointed him to the faculty of the department of architecture, and in the course of the 1940s and 1950s, Caldwell left his imprint on the campus. Nearly everything he achieved is apparent today but largely on account of the restorative efforts of later designers; over the years many plantings were lost, and in 1999 IIT undertook a landscape master plan in order to recreate Caldwell's work and enhance it appropriately.

The process began with the hiring of the landscape architect Michael van Valkenburgh of Cambridge, Massachusetts, in a supervisory capacity. Some of what has been accomplished is traceable to his concepts, but most has been carried out by his successor, Peter Lindsay Schaudt of Chicago. The new landscape followed the avowed intention of the master plan to leave the viewer with a perceptible sense of a "campus in a park." This meant drawing attention to the local greenery and adding to it, while de-emphasizing all that interfered with it—most notably, the automobile.

Parkway on State Street between Thirty-first and Thirty-fifth streets

The parkways on State Street between Thirty-first and Thirty-fifth streets were widened and the street itself narrowed, with curbside parking eliminated. The decision to plant more than 350 trees on the median as well as on both the east and west parkways was inspired by a small stand of honey locusts that had been left by Caldwell directly east of Crown Hall.

Schaudt's team has given most of the remainder of its energy to the landscape west of State Street, especially north of Crown Hall. There approximately seventy-five trees have been planted, and students of landscape architecture can easily recognize that they are native to the area, a sign of Schaudt's faithfulness to Caldwell and of Caldwell's allegiance to the prairie school of landscape architecture, specifically its leading practitioner, Jens Jensen. The species of the trees bear out these relationships: native honey locust, catalpa, elm, and hackberry, with red buds sometimes growing beneath their taller neighbors.

Caldwell's preference for trees placed naturally rather than in straight, predetermined rows also accounts for the freedom of arboreal arrangements observable throughout the campus. Further attention in the space north of Crown Hall has been paid to the lawn, which covers the site of a Mies-designed classroom building never built because of insufficient funds. There the earth has been lowered by about two feet. Spring bulbs have been planted along the periphery, and the walls have been beveled so that spectators can sit casually along the borders. The north end of the lawn is called the Galvin-Pritzker Grove, the name engraved on the long bench that overlooks it. The lindens growing in front of Main Hall were planted by Skidmore, Owings & Merrill in the early 1960s, following the completion of Hermann Hall and Galvin Library. Schaudt and his colleagues decided to remove the lower branches in order to allow more sunshine to wash the ground. They also installed limestone benches in the area and laid down crushed granite. Elsewhere, pink concrete campus sidewalks west of State Street that Mies himself had specified have been restored. And pedestrian lights now illuminate the walks bordering the main east-west axis

TOP: *Galvin–Pritzker Grove*
BOTTOM: *Plaza across from Main Building*

Field north of Crown Hall

of the campus, Thirty-third Street, where more plantings have lately
taken root.

     Morton Park, the one area at IIT that needed no substantial addition
or change, lies north of Hermann Hall. There Caldwell's plantings, so placed
as to leave a rectangular meadow nipped in slightly on the long side, are
still intact. The latter-day landscape architects have been content to leave it
as is and simply provide it with appropriate care.

Illinois Institute of Technology owes most of the buildings on its main campus to a man born at a time and place that had little to do with technology in the modern sense. His name was Maria Ludwig Michael Mies, and the members of his immediate family made their living as stonemasons, chiefly as craftsmen of tombstones. He was born in the Rhineland city of Aachen in 1886, shortly after the creation of a unified imperial Germany. Some thirty-five years later, he renamed himself Ludwig Mies van der Rohe, eventually becoming one of the world's most illustrious architects, with a reputation that depended in no small way on his master plan for the campus of Armour Institute of Technology (later IIT) and his design of the major buildings occupying that site, which still draw pilgrims from around the world.

These remarks recount Mies's life and extraordinary career, including details of his work for IIT, as well as the educational role he played at that university after it persuaded him to emigrate from Germany and assume the chair of its department of architecture in 1938.

The Aachen of Mies's youth was a provincial city, but one that looked back upon a glorious past. It had been the capital of Charlemagne's empire, the first great state in Europe following the fall of the Roman Empire. Charlemagne reigned at the turn of the ninth century, and Mies recalled sitting as a child in the splendid chapel that had been built for the emperor in 800 A.D. by another historically important designer, Odo of Metz. One of the most advanced structures of its time, the chapel served as the site of the coronation of German kings from the tenth to the sixteenth centuries. It was constructed of powerful stonework, an attribute that no doubt especially impressed the child of a professional stonemason.

Mies's parents were Roman Catholics, as was customary in that part of Germany. They were conservative in their beliefs and competent at their trade, although they had little ambition to rise economically above the craftsman class and even less taste for matters of the intellect. Thus the education of young Mies—known as a child by the name Ludwig—was modest, consisting of elementary school followed by the Aachen cathedral school and later by courses in the local trade school. He was the youngest of five children, and since tradition had it that his brother Ewald, the eldest, would one day take over the family business, Ludwig in his teens worked as an apprentice on local building sites, where he learned to assist in drawing plans, the closest he came to training in architecture. While the city boasted a major architectural school, his family did not have the means to send him there. Nonetheless, he was a remarkably capable draftsman, with a skill that earned him assignments in the offices of several local architects. One of them had been commissioned to design a department store in Aachen, but the client decided to turn the project over to a Berlin firm, whose architects, engineers, and clerical staff soon took up places in the office of the original architect, now demoted to associate. Continuing work in the studio as a draftsman, Mies impressed the newcomers, one of whom encouraged him to seek his fortunes in the German capital. A search of the classified ads in a professional journal and subsequent application led to a job in the municipal building department of the Berlin suburb of Rixdorf. That term of service lasted until he enrolled the following year in the School of Art of the Berlin Museum of Industrial and Applied Arts, run by a well-known furniture designer lately turned architect, Bruno Paul. Mies was accepted as a student, but Paul, impressed by what the young man had learned from his experience on the Aachen scaffolds, invited him to work at the same time, professionally, in Paul's studio.

Shortly thereafter Mies was approached by a woman who had earlier used Paul's services and who now claimed to be looking for a gifted neophyte architect to design a country house for her and her husband, Alois Riehl, a distinguished professor of philosophy in the Friedrich Wilhelm University in Berlin. Mies offered himself, and although Mrs. Riehl expressed concern about his lack of professional experience, he was persuasive enough to gain the commission. He was twenty-one when he saw his design of a residence for the Riehls, his first independent work, completed in 1907 in Potsdam. Though less innovative than reliant on local Brandenburgian tradition, the house was striking in the logic of the plan and the unity of its two primary elevations, one overlooking a flat, formal garden, the other an informally planted slope with a welcome view of a lake in the distance.

The house garnered praise from critics of several leading journals. Yet no less important to Mies's later career, the Riehls found him personally attractive, partly because of his quiet but natural magnetism, and partly because of Mies's interest in philosophy, developed on his own, that appealed to the professor. He was regularly invited to receptions at the new house that were attended by the social and intellectual elite of Berlin. There he was introduced to a number of people of both consequence and wherewithal who would later grant him residential commissions of their own.

But that would have to wait. Persuaded that he still needed experience with an established architect to further his career, he secured employment in 1908 with one of Germany's most famous designers, Peter Behrens. This was a prudent move by Mies, who proved himself sufficiently accomplished to rise in the hierarchy of Behrens's office and to participate in several important public and residential projects. In fact, when Behrens was commissioned by the Dutch industrialist A. J. Kröller and his wife Helene Kröller-Müller to design a house large enough to accommodate their huge art collection, Mies was made his boss's chief assistant on the project. As matters developed, Mrs. Kröller-Müller did not respond favorably to Behrens's design and Mies was asked to submit a proposal of his own. This too failed to win approval; indeed, it led finally to an unfriendly breakup with Behrens. But it was by far the most assured design Mies had produced until then, as is confirmed by photographs of the model that have appeared in most of the studies dealing with Mies's early career. It also provided him with the experience and confidence to begin his own practice once and for all, in 1912.

Upon his return to Berlin in the same year, he resumed a relationship he had earlier formed with Ada Bruhn, a gifted, comely, well-to-do young woman whom he had met at one of the receptions at the Riehls'. The couple was married in 1913 and took up residence in Lichterfelde, a Berlin suburb. Since Mies's financial condition was less than robust, they depended heavily on Ada's family wealth, which provided a foundation for his professional practice.

While history often identifies Mies as one of the principal innovators of the modernist movement, virtually everything he produced in the years immediately following his marriage was stylistically traditional. The influence of Behrens is apparent, as is that of Karl Friedrich Schinkel, whose work Mies learned to know largely because Behrens admired it. Schinkel was by consensus the greatest nineteenth-century German architect, and while he designed with equal command in the Neogothic and the neoclassical, it was the latter mode that had drawn increased attention among the nation's better-informed architects during Mies's formative years. In view of that, it can be argued that Mies's approach to design was, if not stylistically radical, surely in the mainstream current of the time.

One of his most impressive early works—like the unbuilt Kröller House—was a design he submitted to a competition for a memorial monument to Otto von Bismarck, the first chancellor of the united Germany, that was intended to be constructed on a bluff overlooking the Rhine. Mies's concept, which consisted of a massive podium anchored in the hillside and extending away from the river to embrace a vast festival field, was almost completely dependent on Behrens's example, but it convincingly conveyed the monumentality appropriate to its ends, and the stunning realism of Mies's presentation drawing demonstrated that he was even a better draftsman in 1910 than he had been when his graphic talent effectively launched his career.

Mies's house designs of the second decade of the century constituted, as it were, a catalog of the influences he drew upon. The Perls House of 1911 is closely modeled on Schinkel's pavilion at Schloss Charlottenburg, while the plan of the 1913 Werner House is perceptibly similar to that of Behrens's Wiegand House. The elevations of the Warnholtz House of 1915—record of which was only recently discovered—are dependent on those of the Oppenheim House, a work by another architect Mies admired—Alfred Messel. The Urbig House of 1915, commissioned by friends of the Riehls, was probably the most ambitious design Mies completed during these years, but it too is marked by devices clearly traceable to Schinkel.

While he was at work on this last commission, Mies was conscripted into the German army. Lacking the kind of education that would prepare him for an officer's commission, he spent well over a year tending to office work at his regimental headquarters in Berlin and was later sent to an engineering unit in Romania, remaining there until the war ended. By early 1919 he had rejoined his family in Berlin.

During the early 1920s Mies's architecture underwent a change of such magnitude that on the surface it bears no relationship to anything he had done earlier. Five projects designed between 1921 and 1924 vaulted him into the front phalanx of the modernist avant-garde, where he remained for the rest of his career in Germany.

Curiously, however, despite all the attention that work has attracted over the years, we know relatively little about how he passed the years just before it. One event worthy of speculation in this connection was his submission of the Kröller project, of which he was justifiably proud, to the 1919 Ausstellung für unbekannte Architekten (Exhibition of unknown architects), a display of recent work sponsored by the Arbeitsrat für Kunst. In charge of the show was Walter Gropius, who had also worked for Behrens but who was far more committed than Mies to the experimental stylistic ideas that were gathering force at the time in all the European arts. Gropius rejected the Kröller project, providing Mies, if he chose to act on it, with reason to take the avant-garde more seriously than he had theretofore. Moreover, changes in his domestic life were pending. Though Ada had given birth to three daughters between 1914 and 1917, the record suggests that Mies was never a responsible father, or as time passed, a devoted husband. Sometime late in 1921 Ada and the children moved into an apartment in the Berlin suburb of Bornstedt. There was no formal divorce, but she and Mies never lived together again. At about this time he also changed his name, by connecting his father's surname and his mother's maiden name with the invented "van der," yielding "Mies van der Rohe."

Each of the five projects of the early 1920s deviated markedly from precedent. The drawing of the Friedrichstrasse Office Building (1921) showed a multistory structure rising like a cliff of glass, vertically notched and horizontally uninterrupted, from the sidewalk to a roofline with no cornice. The model of the Glass Skyscraper (1922) also promised height, but instead of sharp angles, the walls were sinuously curved, clad again in glass, with the only surface incident taking the form of slender lineaments that marked the divisions between floors.

In the Concrete Office Building (1923) Mies used that characteristically modern industrial material in the service of a new image. Floor slabs turning upward at the building edge alternated with spaces through which ceiling beams could be seen from the street. Such an open and closed composition was altogether new, and it offered an early example of an elevation that prefigured the modernist device—the ribbon window—that surrounds the building without interruption. Mies felt strongly enough about this project that he published a statement in a journal called *G* summing up his rationale for it: "Reinforced concrete buildings are by nature skeletal constructions. No gingerbread, no armored towers. With columns and girders, no loadbearing walls. That is to say, skin and bones building." The words were a compact expression of a building philosophy that he would embrace for the rest of his life.

The last of the five projects were two country houses, one of concrete and one of brick, notable for Mies's novel treatment of circulation. The brick country house featured freestanding interior walls that defined rather than enclosed space, forming an open plan that went beyond anything proposed until then.

The friends Mies made while he was busy with these new works tended to be members of the Berlin artistic and architectural avant-garde, and in that circle his name was taken ever more seriously. Even so, he maintained his connections with the clientele he had relied on before the war ended. The Mosler House, designed in 1924 and built in Neubabelsberg close to several of his other houses, was as conservative in manner as anything he had conceived earlier. It was, however, the last of its type. By the middle of the 1920s he had become involved in professional organizations like the Bund deutscher Architekten (Association of German Architects) and the Deutscher Werkbund, which would help to advance his career. His work veered from earlier uses of tradition, and in the Wolf House of 1926 he committed himself to the design of outer walls with large, unornamented, cleanly framed windows, and in the interior, to a plan affected by the openness of his earlier brick country house as well as that project's proposed material.

The Wolf House was built of load-bearing brick, a substance that reminds us of Mies's early life as the member of a craftsman's family. In the late 1920s he effected a unity between brick and modernist composition, most prominently in another memorial monument, one that was realized, in 1926, in a Berlin cemetery. Commissioned by German communists and dedicated to the party's fallen heroes Karl Liebknecht and Rosa Luxemburg, the finished work was a mass of interlocking blocks in clinker brick that bore no iconographical similarity with past memorials. Mies followed this design several years later with a pair of houses in the Rhineland city of Krefeld, the Lange House and the Esters House, both comparable to the Wolf House in the modernity of exterior and interior treatment—and both of brick.

By the end of the 1920s and the completion of those two houses, Mies had taken his place among the leaders of the movement known as Neues Bauen (new building), which stood for the modernist position, lately grown international in scope. It was an event of 1927 that proved the importance of this development, and Mies was largely responsible for it. In 1925 the Deutscher Werkbund appointed him artistic director of an exhibition of houses to be built on the Weissenhof, a hill overlooking the city of Stuttgart. Two years later the exhibition, which was made up of a group of dwellings designed by the foremost modernists of the day, opened to the public. Houses by Mies, Gropius, Behrens, Hans Scharoun, Ludwig Hilberseimer, Bruno and Max Taut, all of Germany, J. J. P. Oud and Mart Stam of Holland, Josef Frank of Austria, Victor Bourgeois of Belgium, and Le Corbusier of France were marked by several shared properties, chief among them flat roofs and white, unornamented facades. The modern movement had become a fact, and the way to the future was in place.

In 1930, three years after the Weissenhof colony opened, Mies accepted the directorship of the famed Bauhaus, a post he held until 1934. His contribution to that school is remembered as less important and innovative than that of Gropius, who founded it in 1919, in Weimar, and later moved it into a building of his own design, in Dessau.

Nonetheless, during his Bauhaus years Mies designed two buildings that are usually regarded as the masterpieces of his European period. The first was a pavilion representing Germany at the Barcelona International Exposition of 1929. Nothing about it abided by historical standards. An assembly of walls and columns covered by a flat roof was erected on a long, narrow stone podium. The freestanding walls were made of uncommonly elegant materials: green marble, travertine, and tinted glass, arranged to address a spectacular wall of golden onyx. The asymmetrical organization of the walls was punctuated by a symmetrical grouping of slim, cruciform columns in chrome, the entire ensemble displaying highly reflective surfaces. The plan was completed by a shallow pool at each end of the pavilion. In the smaller one stood a slightly larger than life statue, *Dawn*, by the German sculptor Georg Kolbe. Since there was effectively no formal entrance to the pavilion, the distinction between exterior and interior was greatly diminished. Nor was there any certain path through it. As a result, the experience of the space, added to that of the lustrous materials, left a singularly memorable impression.

Even as the pavilion was being completed, Mies was at work on the design of a house for Fritz and Grete Tugendhat, a Czech couple who owned a plot of sloping land in the city of Brno. Once completed there, in 1930, the house expressed a one-story elevation on the street side and a two-story elevation overlooking the landscape to the rear. The upper floor was given over to sleeping quarters with access to a terrace that also served as the roof of the lower floor. Thus both stories enjoyed a handsome view of lawn and trees. The main living space was a marvelous open plan, with the parlor divided from the study by another splendid onyx wall, and from the dining room by a semicylindrical wall of macassar ebony. The slope was visible from the parlor on the south through a glass wall, eighty feet in length, whose alternate panes could be lowered, as an automobile window is lowered. Another glass wall to the east, some fifty-five feet long, separated the parlor from a winter garden. This very description suggests that Mies worked with a handsome budget, which he justified by the excellence of his materials and particularly by the furniture he designed, several examples of which have since become classics. Nor were these efforts his first in that medium. Just as he had designed furniture in the traditional manner for some of his early clients, he produced a chair for his apartment block at the Weissenhof colony and, later, the ultimately world-renowned chair for the Barcelona Pavilion.

The 1920s were about to end on a triumphant note for Mies when a series of reverses occurred that turned the next decade into the worst of his life. The Great Depression was the first of these misfortunes, and in a sense the parent of the others. The German economy collapsed and set into motion social and political turbulence that finally led, in 1933, to the takeover of the government by the National Socialists under Adolf Hitler. Quarrels within the Nazi party over the policies it should adopt toward the arts were settled soon enough in favor of tradition and in opposition to the modernist point of view. Mies found his career in jeopardy, not only because the Depression robbed him of possible new clients but because the new government did not look fondly on the architecture he had been responsible for. A few of his house designs of the 1930s were realized, but they were modest at best, while several, like the Gericke House of 1931 and the Hubbe House of 1935, were among his most inspired endeavors, but for a variety of reasons, were never built. The Bauhaus itself, under pressure from right-wing elements, had moved in 1932 from Dessau to Berlin, but the following year the faculty, recognizing that the school had no future in Germany under the Nazis, decided to close its doors for good.

Mies was in effect rescued by people in the United States who already knew and admired him. The process began when a New York advertising executive commissioned him to design a house for a site in Wyoming. Mies made the trip there from Germany, staying long enough to commence work on the design. While returning to New York, he stopped in Chicago to confer with authorities at the Armour Institute of Technology (AIT) who had asked him to consider appointment to the chair of the school's department of architecture. He accepted on the spot.

Armour's approach to architectural education had long been based on beaux-arts principles, which had emphasized instruction of students in the historical styles and in rendering images of them in a highly pictorialized manner. In view of the recent success of the new European architecture, much of which was stylistically ahistoricist, the beaux-arts seemed increasingly passé, leading Armour to search for someone who could formulate a radically new educational system. Under Mies's direction, the Armour curriculum was changed accordingly, with attention directed to visual training in the abstract, to the slow, careful study of materials and purposes, and only later to the design of whole buildings and to the study of urbanism. To assist in this process, Mies invited two former Bauhaus colleagues, Ludwig Hilberseimer and Walter Peterhans, to join the AIT faculty.

Mies assumed his professorial duties in the fall of 1938. In the following year he was asked to develop a master plan for the university's campus, concentrated at the intersection of Federal and Thirty-third streets. This request was another part of the plan to alter the character of the entire school. In 1935 the Board of Trustees decided to extend the limits of the campus by buying nearby land, and by 1937 thirty-one acres had been added to an area encompassing six city blocks, from Thirty-first to Thirty-fifth streets along State Street and west to the tracks of the Rock Island Railroad (later named the New York Central).

The Chicago firm of Holabird & Root had already proposed a master plan in 1937, before Mies was formally appointed. The likelihood that Mies would produce something more stylistically advanced, as well as buildings of his own design, appealed to AIT president Henry Heald, who was eager to do all he could to modernize the school. Even so, while Mies obviously stood for modernity, he had much to learn about a country he hardly knew, about its language, culture, and building methods. He later recalled that assumption of the campus plan was the "biggest decision I ever had to make."

He began his assignment by studying classroom and laboratory requirements and, based on what he learned in the process, by laying down a square grid over the whole campus. His chosen module measured twenty-four by twenty-four feet—a standard bay size—with a twelve-foot height. Most of the buildings completed to his designs conformed to those ordering dimensions.

His earliest sketches postulated an axis—Thirty-third Street—with a library on one side and a student union on the other. In the course of the next seven years he experimented constantly, plotting different arrangements of buildings, individual building plans, elevations, materials, profiles, heights, and sites—with the library and student union consistently given pride of place across the Thirty-third Street corridor. No less important was his treatment of the trees and green space surrounding the contemplated buildings. He was assisted in this regard by the landscape architect Alfred Caldwell, who was a student at IIT and later an IIT professor. Also notable in the scheme that he had worked out by the end of 1939 were classroom buildings with auditoriums and stairwells extruded from the main mass. Drawings showing assorted plans for the student union indicate that he was considering the use of overhead trusses to keep an interior auditorium free of columns—a gesture that hinted at his later development of clear span buildings. Even so, he sometimes harked back to habits of his German period, most memorably in sketches showing cruciform columns reminiscent of those used in the Barcelona Pavilion.

During 1940 Mies was at work on a second plan, in which he simplified and clarified both the spatial composition of campus buildings and the masses of classroom buildings, tucking stairwells and auditoriums (where needed) within the walls. In January 1941, having been at work on the entire project for a year and a half, he was informed by Heald that the trustees had decided instead to make a public presentation of a master scheme prepared by another Chicago architect (and board trustee), Alfred Alschuler, before he died, late in 1940. Heald, aware that Mies was taken aback by his message, added a mollifying note:

> I do not want you to feel that, because the Board is using Mr. Alschuler's sketch, it represents any reflection on your work in connection with the program. It happens that [Alschuler] had prepared a sketch which shows a partial development with certain old buildings in use and which is not as comprehensive as the general program on which you have been working, and the Board felt that at this time it would be best to show the picture in that way.

Regardless of this contretemps Mies persisted in his efforts, and in the course of 1941 the situation changed in his favor. In October Heald announced that the Mies plan was intact, approved and awaiting completion.

By 1947 he was finished with the master plan. However, not all of the buildings he had planned were realized. The most grievous loss was the library, surely the most monumental design he ever produced for the university and among the grandest of his career. The chief consolation lay in the buildings he did see completed. Among these, S. R. Crown Hall (1956), which serves to this day as the school of architecture, is the most important, not least because its freedom from interior columns qualified it as his first clear-span structure on a large scale. And the master plan itself, though less fulfilled than intended, was realized to a degree that leaves IIT with one of the most spatially provocative campus plans in the United States. Mies did manage to retain the symmetrically ordering axis of Thirty-third Street, and on either side the buildings he completed a free layout that provided an innovative urbanistic note to the streetscape of Chicago.

Mies retired from IIT in 1958, almost a half century ago. Yet to this day his image remains bright in the minds of the architecture faculty and students, indeed of the university as a whole. Surely central to this are the twenty-two campus buildings he produced and the shape of the educational program he initiated. But the world beyond the campus recalls Mies no less vividly, for different reasons. During his tenure at IIT, he carried on a practice in which he not only sustained the reputation he brought with him from Germany but added to it with a series of masterworks that had few equals in the modern period. Shortly after he arrived in Chicago he had the good fortune to meet Herbert Greenwald, a developer who enabled him to design a pair of apartment towers on Chicago's elegant Lake Shore Drive that, once finished in 1951, became the cynosure of the international architecture world. The two rectangular slabs, inventively sited on a trapezoidal lot, were built of steel with floor-to-ceiling windows of glass, a construction that revolutionized high-rise buildings in post–World War II America. In the same year he produced a private house that was in its way as masterly as his Tugendhat House of 1930 and even more innovative: the Farnsworth House, a superbly proportioned unitary space framed in steel with enclosing walls of glass. As columns of the house Mies employed a wide-flange beam, a device that became virtually his signature building element in the 1950s and 1960s.

He followed this commission with a skyscraper for New York, the Seagram Building of 1958. He was once again granted a lavish budget, to which he responded by cladding the building in that most patrician of metals: bronze. Moreover, he set the structure back from Park Avenue, leaving a spacious plaza that included a pair of shallow pools. The Seagram Building is still regarded by many observers as the most distinguished address in the United States.

Despite these various successes, Mies saw some of his most ambitious American projects fail realization. Mention has already been made of the unbuilt library at IIT. Of comparable quality were two designs of the early 1950s. One was an entry submitted in 1953 to a competition for a National Theater in Mannheim. Mies proposed a building that would have housed two auditoriums of different sizes as well as auxiliary spaces. Like Crown Hall, the structure would have relied on overhead supports—not plate girders, as at Crown Hall, but open trusses. Considerably larger than Crown Hall, the theater would have been surpassed in size by the colossal Convention Hall of 1954, which was meant to be 720 square feet in plan, covering over 500,000 square feet in floor area, with an interior height of 85 feet. To keep the interior free of columns, Mies conceived a roof structure consisting of 30-foot-deep two-directional steel trusses on 30-foot centers. These dimensions surpassed anything else in Mies's catalog.

Another unbuilt project, the Bacardi Office Building of 1958, meant for Santiago, Cuba, furnished the idea from which Mies derived his last major completed work, the Neue National Galerie, an art museum finished in 1967 in Berlin. In final form the square-shaped interior hall was walled totally in glass, with the roof consisting of an orthogonal grid of web girders six feet deep spaced at twelve-foot intervals. Eight flanged cruciform steel columns painted black, two to a side, met the roof at its edge. Mies himself, returned at last to the city where he had established himself decades before, was in attendance when the roof was raised by hydraulic jacks set at the points along the perimeter where the columns were later erected.

During the 1950s and much of the 1960s Mies van der Rohe had become arguably the most influential living architect. The skylines of the world's leading cities repeated the rectilinearities standard in his own high rises, although that very commonalty led to a movement organized in opposition to him and the other modernists of his generation. It was known as postmodernism, and simply put, it sought to return to buildings the trappings of historical form that modernist abstraction had abandoned. As a consequence Mies's reputation suffered in the 1970s and 1980s, yet postmodernism failed to produce anything that surpassed Mies's work, and his reputation was fully restored by the turn of the century.

The memorial service following Mies's death in 1969 took place in a setting that could not have been more appropriate: Crown Hall, a building of his own design that served Illinois Institute of Technology, as well as his host city, Chicago, and host country, the United States, as surely as it did the international architectural community.

Franz Schulze

Selected Bibliography

Achilles, Rolf, Kevin Harrington, and Charlotte Myhrum, eds. *Mies van der Rohe: Architect as Educator*. Chicago: Illinois Institute of Technology, Mies van der Rohe Centennial Project, 1986.

Lambert, Phyllis, ed. *Mies in America*. New York: Harry N. Abrams, 2001.

Neumeyer, Fritz. *The Artless Word: Mies van der Rohe on the Building Art*. Cambridge, Massachusetts: MIT Press, 1991.

Schulze, Franz. *Mies van der Rohe: A Critical Biography*. Chicago: University of Chicago Press, 1985.

GEOGRAPHICS

EARTH'S RESOURCES

Izzi Howell

W
FRANKLIN WATTS
LONDON•SYDNEY

Franklin Watts

First published in Great Britain in 2018 by The Watts Publishing Group

Copyright © The Watts Publishing Group 2018

Produced for Franklin Watts by
White-Thomson Publishing Ltd
www.wtpub.co.uk
01273 479982

Series Editor: Izzi Howell
Series Designer: Rocket Design (East Anglia) Ltd

Getty: Askold Romanov 9bl, apomares 11, timoph 21t, Nelson Ching/Bloomberg 28b; Shutterstock: Bukhavets Mikhail 4-5, ArtisticPhoto 5t, boyphare 6, Designua 8, 22 and 23t, Christian Vinces 9t, Mikadun 9br, VectorPot 10, Andrew Rybalko 12, KYTan 13, pupunkkop 15, Richard Thornton 17, Nucleartist 18, Syndromeda 19, Pretty Vectors 20t, humphery 20b, travelpeter 22b, Bernhard Staehli 23b, Faber14 24t, SkyPics Studio 24b, Constantine Androsoff 25t, KittyVector 25bl, Bukhavets Mikhail 25br, MikeDotta 26t, Crystal Eye Studio 26b, OVKNHR 27, avian 28t, canadastock 29.

All design elements from Shutterstock, including Alfmaler, sergio34, sub job, DRogatnev, NadiiaZ, kolotuschenko, petovarga, A7880S, Doloves, Meilun and Alex Oakenman.

ISBN 978 1 4451 5557 9

Printed in China

MIX
Paper from
responsible sources
FSC® C104740
www.fsc.org
FSC

Franklin Watts
An imprint of
Hachette Children's Group
Part of The Watts Publishing Group
Carmelite House
50 Victoria Embankment
London EC4Y 0DZ

An Hachette UK Company
www.hachette.co.uk
www.franklinwatts.co.uk

Contents

What are Resources?

There are many natural resources on Earth that we can use to make objects, support ourselves or produce energy. Wood, metal and stone are used for construction. Fossil fuels, running water and sunlight can be used to produce electricity.

Renewable resources

Wind, sunlight and water are described as renewable resources. Our supply of these resources will naturally renew, no matter how much we use of them. Wood and other resources that can be regrown quickly and easily are also renewable. However, humans have to make sure they replant and replace these resources, so that they have a supply in the future.

Radioactive material (page 27)

Rubber (page 12)

Coal (page 8)

Metal (page 8)

Stone (page 8)

Precious stones (page 8)

We currently extract

60,000 billion kg

of natural resources from Earth every year.

Non-renewable resources

Many resources on Earth, such as coal, oil and minerals, are non-renewable. Once we use up our supply of these resources, it will take millions of years for the resources to naturally form again.

At the moment, we have enough oil to last us for around 50 more years.

Oil wells pump oil from reserves deep underground.

Animals (page 18)

Wood (page 12)

Plants (page 18)

Gas (page 22)

Oil (page 22)

Water (page 16)

Using resources

It's important that humans use resources in a responsible and sustainable way. We need to share resources fairly so that everyone on Earth has access to the resources that they need. Restricting our use of some resources will allow us to leave enough for future generations. We also need to be careful that we do not gather or process resources in a way that harms the natural environment.

Resources Around the World

Some countries consume far more resources than others. The amount of resources used by a country depends on its income.

Different incomes

High-income countries use the most resources. People in these countries own more objects and live in bigger houses that consume more energy. They eat more food and use more water than people in low and middle-income countries.

x1

x10

People in high-income countries use

10 times

more resources than people in low-income countries.

Gathering resources

Many resources are extracted in low and middle-income countries. People gather raw materials, such as minerals, timber and crops. These jobs are known as primary sector jobs. People who work in primary sector jobs often earn low salaries and work long hours in difficult conditions.

This man in Thailand is cutting down a large tree into smaller planks of wood.

Processing resources

Once a resource has been gathered, it needs to be processed into a product that we can use. For example, planks of wood are cut from logs and plastic is made from oil. People who process resources work in the secondary sector. Building objects from materials, such as making a car from metal and plastic, is also a secondary sector job.

Managing resources

Tertiary sector jobs deal with the management of resources. Some people who work in the tertiary sector own the factories that process resources, organise the shipping of resources or sell them to other people. These jobs are relatively well paid. They are often done by people who live in high-income countries.

Main export of countries

This map shows the main resource/material export of countries around the world.

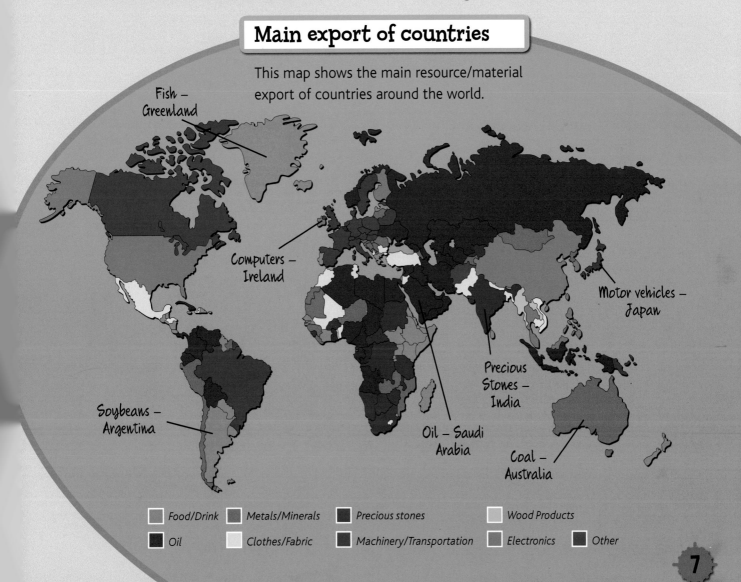

Fish – Greenland

Computers – Ireland

Motor vehicles – Japan

Precious Stones – India

Soybeans – Argentina

Oil – Saudi Arabia

Coal – Australia

Food/Drink   Metals/Minerals   Precious stones   Wood Products

Oil   Clothes/Fabric   Machinery/Transportation   Electronics   Other

Mining

Mining is the removal of rocks and minerals from the surface of the Earth. Stone for construction, precious gems, such as diamonds, and different metals are all collected through mining.

Uses

Mined resources are used in many ways. As well as construction, different metals are used in mobile phones, TVs, lightbulbs and computers. Drills for cutting bricks and concrete sometimes have diamond tips. Gold pieces are often used in electrical circuits.

Surface mining

One of the simplest types of mining is surface mining. Miners remove layers of soil and rock to access deeper layers that contain valuable resources, such as coal. The hole created is called a quarry. Surface mining is easiest for miners, as they do not have to work deep underground. Rocks such as limestone and marble are usually cut from quarries.

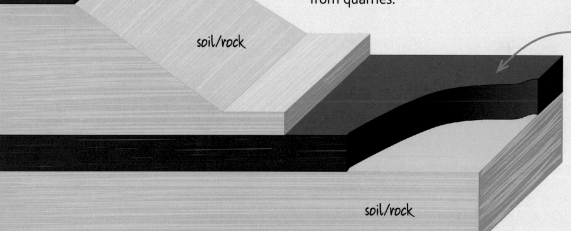

soil/rock

coal

soil/rock

Quarries can be seen cut into the hillside.

Underground mining

Some resources can only be gathered from underground mines. Miners use machines to dig tunnels to access resources buried deep below the surface. In the past, miners had to dig all underground tunnels and cut away rock by hand. They worked in dangerous, hot conditions. Today, conditions in underground mines are better, but in some countries, miners still work in unsafe tunnels.

These miners in Bolivia are placing explosives that will blow up a section of the rock wall. Then, they will transport the smaller pieces of rock for processing.

Processing

Many resources that come from mines have to be processed before they can be used. Some metals combine with other minerals to make ores. To remove a metal from an ore, the ore is heated until the metal separates from the other minerals.

Environmental impact

Mining can have a negative impact on the environment. Surface mines destroy the habitats of many animals and plants. If underground mines are not supported properly, they can collapse inwards, creating a sinkhole. The chemicals used in mining and waste from ore processing are often dumped nearby and not cleaned up properly. They poison the land and the water supply, causing great harm to plants, animals and humans.

The water in this lake has been polluted by copper mining.

Aluminium

Aluminium is a soft, lightweight metal that is often used in vehicles and buildings. It is a common metal, making up around 8 per cent of the Earth's crust.

Uses

Aluminium is a very useful metal, as it is strong and flexible and does not rust. It is commonly used to make aircraft and trains, as well as window frames. Most people have aluminium food and drinks cans and aluminium foil in their homes.

Ore

Aluminium is rarely found in its pure form. It is a very reactive metal and it nearly always reacts with other minerals to form an ore – bauxite. Bauxite forms close to the surface, so miners extract it from quarries, rather than tunnelling underground.

Location

Bauxite ore is found all over the world. The largest bauxite mines are in Australia, Brazil, China and Guinea. In these countries, bauxite quarries have destroyed large areas of rainforest and other natural habitats.

In this bauxite mine in Venezuela, large areas of the tree-covered mountains have been stripped away so that miners can access the bauxite underneath.

Processing bauxite

Extracting aluminium from bauxite is a complicated process that uses a lot of electricity. Some companies build processing plants in areas with cheap electricity, such as Iceland, which gets 'free' electricity from geothermal energy (see page 25). However, many processing plants run on fossil fuels, which damage the environment.

Recycling aluminium only requires

5 per cent

of the energy that it takes to make new aluminium from bauxite ore. For this reason, it is much better for the environment for us to recycle aluminium.

Recycling

Recycling aluminium uses far less electricity than creating new aluminium. To recycle aluminium, old aluminium products are melted down and formed into sheets. These sheets are then used to make new products. Recycling aluminium also means that less bauxite needs to be mined, which causes less damage to the environment.

Wood

Wood is a common resource that can be used in many different ways. Our supply of wood must be carefully managed, as removing too many trees can harm the natural environment.

Uses

We can use pieces of wood to build houses and furniture. We can also burn wood as a fuel. There are resources in other parts of a tree, such as its fruit and its sap. Sap from the maple tree can be made into maple syrup and sap from the rubber tree can be processed into rubber.

Processing

Wood used for building is called timber. Some logs are cut by hand using chain saws. Other wood is cut to size by huge industrial saws in a timber mill. The sawdust and scraps of woods that are left behind are glued together to make chipboard. Chipboard is much cheaper than wood, but it isn't as strong.

Deforestation

People cut down around 15 billion trees every year. Some of this wood is used as a resource, while some woodland areas are cleared so that the land can be used in other ways. Many woodland areas are cleared to make room for agriculture. When a forest is cut down and not replanted with trees, it is known as deforestation.

Replanting

Some cleared forest areas are replanted with more trees. In doing so, we can guarantee our supply of wood for the future. However, many areas are not replanted with the same trees that were cut down. People plant fast-growing trees, such as pines, that will quickly grow big enough to be cut down again. Rubber and palm trees, from which rubber and palm oil can be gathered, are also popular trees to plant.

Biodiversity

When people cut down forests and plant different species of trees in their place, it destroys the forest ecosystem. The new trees may not provide the right habitat or type of food for forest animals. Most old forests are very biodiverse, with lots of species of plants and animals. This biodiversity is lost when only one species of tree is replanted.

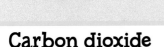

This area has been cleared of woodland to plant new palm trees for palm oil.

Carbon dioxide

Replanting trees helps the environment. Trees, and all plants, absorb carbon dioxide (CO_2). If we cut down trees without replanting them, there will be fewer trees to absorb carbon dioxide and so the level of carbon dioxide in the atmosphere will go up. This has a negative impact on the climate of the Earth (see page 23).

One tree absorbs around 22 kg of CO_2 every year.

That's the same amount as one car releases by driving 18 km.

It would take 706 trees to absorb the average amount of CO_2 released by one car in the UK every year.

FOCUS ON

Rainforest Deforestation

Deforestation happens all over the world but tropical rainforests are some of the most affected areas. If the current rate of deforestation continues, we will destroy all the rainforests within the next one hundred years.

Tropical hardwood

Loggers cut down rainforest trees such as mahogany, ebony and teak. The wood from these trees is valued for its beauty and strength and can be sold for a much higher price than other types of wood. Many loggers work illegally, gathering more wood than they are allowed to. They destroy large areas of rainforest to build roads to reach the trees.

One m³
of mahogany is worth over
£1,200.

Rainforest resources

Rainforests are home to many valuable resources besides wood, including fruits, nuts and spices. Many rainforest plants are used in life-saving medicines, such as those that treat cancer. Some farmers plant coffee, banana and avocado trees among wild rainforest trees without damaging the natural habitat. If a product has a Rainforest Alliance label, it means that it has been grown in a sustainable way.

Slash and burn

Many farmers clear rainforests using a technique called slash and burn. They chop down the rainforest trees and plants and then burn them. The ash from the burned plants fertilises the soil so it is suitable for crops. However, the soil only stays fertile for a few years. If farmers cannot afford fertiliser for their fields, they abandon their land and clear more space through slash and burn.

Burning plants and trees releases carbon dioxide. This leads to global warming (see page 23).

This land in Thailand has been cleared through slash and burn.

Cattle farming

Large areas of rainforest in South America are cleared to make room for cattle farms. Meat from the cattle raised on these farms is sent to shops across South America. Some of it is shipped to other continents around the world. However, cleared rainforest land is not a particularly good place for cows to live. Grass does not grow well in the poor rainforest soil so food has to be brought in for the cows to eat.

Over 60%
of rainforest land that is cleared in Brazil is used for cattle farming.

The future

The governments of some countries are working hard to preserve the rainforests and stop their resources from being destroyed. The Brazilian government has promised to replant over 120,000 square km of rainforest by 2030. Other governments are working to stop illegal logging and to protect the habitats of rainforest plants and animals.

Water

Water is one of the most important resources on Earth. We use water in many ways – in our homes, on farms and in different industries. However, there are many people around the world who do not have access to a clean, reliable water supply.

Water on Earth

Over 70 per cent of the Earth's surface is covered in water. However, most of this water is salt water. Only 3 per cent of the water on Earth is fresh water, which we can use for drinking, household use and agriculture.

Uses

High-income countries use much more water than other low and middle-income countries. People in high-income countries use more water in their homes than people in other countries. They have access to baths, washing machines and dishwashers, all of which consume water. In low-income countries, most water is used in agriculture to irrigate the fields.

Amount of water used per person per day:

USA: 590 litres a day

India: 144 litres a day

Mali: 11 litres a day

Gathering water

People gather water from above and below the ground. Fresh water can be taken from lakes, rivers and reservoirs (artificial lakes). Water also soaks through the ground and fills the space between soil and rocks. This water can be accessed through springs or by digging a well.

Safe water

Water often needs to be processed so that it is safe for humans to drink or use. It is filtered and mixed with chemicals that kill dangerous bacteria. This process is also used to clean dirty water that leaves our homes through sewage pipes. Once this dirty water has been cleaned, it can be released back into rivers and lakes.

Drought

We will never run out of water, as it is a renewable resource. However, global warming (see page 23) and our growing population put pressure on our supply of water. Changes to our climate mean that many places are experiencing drought. Less rain means that it is harder for farmers to irrigate their crops. It can also be hard for farmers to find enough water to irrigate the huge fields of crops needed to support a large population.

Some crops, such as almond trees, require much more water than other crops. It takes 5 litres of water to grow just one almond.

Access to water

In high-income countries, most homes are connected to a safe drinking water supply. However, many people in low and middle-income countries have to travel a long way to access water. In some cases, their only water supply may be untreated, dirty water from a river or lake. Drinking dirty water leads to many dangerous, and even fatal, diseases.

Building water pumps near to towns and villages makes it easier for people in low and middle-income countries to gather clean water.

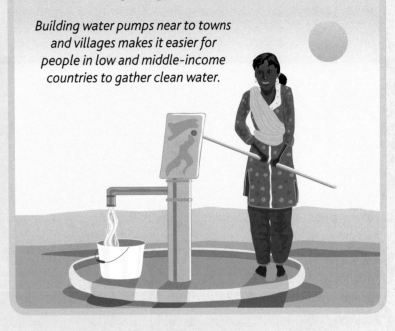

Reducing water use

Using less water saves money and is good for the environment. Some ways of using less water in the home are collecting rainwater to water plants, fixing leaks and fitting toilets that run on recycled bathwater. In industry, factories can reuse water. We can also stop wasting water on non-essential uses, such as watering the grass on golf courses to keep it green.

Food and Farms

There are not enough wild plants and animals on Earth to provide food for our population. Instead, we grow crops and raise animals on farms.

History

The first humans were hunter-gatherers, who moved from place to place looking for wild food to eat. They could not find enough food to support a large number of people, so the human population was small. When humans began to settle in one place and grow food on farms, they could produce large amounts of food. This allowed the human population on Earth to grow much bigger.

Grains

Wheat, rice, corn and other grains are some of the most commonly grown crops around the world. These foods make up the main part of many people's diets. They provide carbohydrates that give people energy. Farmers often use tractors to clear their fields, plant seeds and harvest their crops.

Livestock

Farmers raise animals such as cows, sheep, pigs and chickens for their meat, milk and eggs. Many farmers keep their livestock in closed barns so that it is easier to feed them. Once the animal is large enough to be killed, it is taken to an abattoir. The meat is then processed and taken to be sold.

Import and export

Crops are not always used to feed the people in the area where they are grown. Many crops are grown in low and middle-income countries and then sold to high-income countries. Farmers make more money by exporting one type of crop than by growing different foods for people in their country. However, sending crops around the world by plane and lorry releases greenhouse gases (see page 23) and pollution.

Many farmers in Tanzania, Africa, grow coffee as a cash crop. A cash crop is a crop grown to make money, rather than to provide food for a community.

Food quality

Some people worry about the quality of food that they buy. Many farmers spray their crops with pesticides so that insects don't eat the plants. Some people believe that these pesticides are dangerous for humans, so they buy organic food that is grown without pesticides. Other people think that it's cruel for farmers to keep livestock in small, enclosed barns, so they buy free range meat and dairy products. Free range animals are allowed to spend some time outside.

Sharing food

Today, there are still many people around the world who do not have access to enough food. However, this is not because we cannot grow enough food for everyone. Instead, it is because we do not share food equally around the world. In some places, a huge amount of uneaten food is thrown away. Other people are not paid enough money to buy food to support themselves.

FOCUS ON

GM Crops

Genetically modifying, or changing, crops is one way of increasing the amount of food we have available. However, some people believe that the risks of GM crops are greater than the benefits.

Changes

Genetically modified (GM) crops are crops that have been changed so that they are easier to grow and less likely to die. They aren't affected by pests, plant diseases or periods without water during droughts. Other GM crops grow bigger than normal crops or produce more fruit. This means that they can feed more people.

Global hunger

Around one in nine people around the world suffers from hunger. In some cases this is because they can't grow enough crops to support themselves or their crops die from a disease. GM crops are one way of helping these people grow enough food to avoid hunger.

Concerns

Some people are worried about GM crops. They aren't sure if planting GM crops is good for the environment or if eating GM crops is safe. They believe that there are other ways to solve world hunger, including sharing resources more fairly and encouraging countries to grow crops for themselves rather than selling them to others.

This rice crop has failed because of drought.

North Sea Fishing

Fish are one of the few wild foods that most people eat. Up until the twentieth century, many species of fish lived in the North Sea. There were large numbers of mackerel, salmon, cod and herring. However, overfishing has damaged the population of fish in this area.

North Sea

Overfishing

Many fishermen in the North Sea use huge trawler nets, which they drag across the water, catching anything in their path. These nets allow them to catch a huge number of fish. In the past, fishermen sometimes caught far more fish than they needed. They didn't leave enough fish to breed and replace those that had been lost. In the following years, there were far fewer fish to catch.

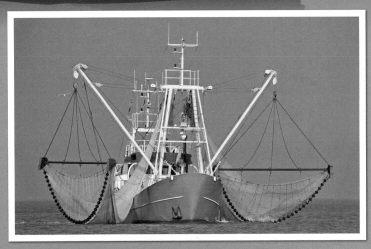

This boat is using a trawler net to fish for crabs in the North Sea.

Consequences

Trawler nets accidentally kill many large ocean animals, such as dolphins and porpoises. They also damage the seabed and kill many ocean plants. When a species of fish has been overfished, it affects the food chain. Predators that usually eat the fish go hungry and can die as well.

Solutions

Some fishermen use special trawler nets that large sea mammals or small young fish can escape from. If fishermen leave the young fish to grow up, their supply of fish is guaranteed for the future. Fish can also be raised on farms, while wild fish populations are left to recover.

Fossil Fuels

Fossil fuels, such as coal, oil and gas, are natural resources that we use for energy. There is a limited amount of fossil fuels left on Earth. They may run out during our lifetime.

Formation and location

Fossil fuels were formed over millions of years from the remains of dead plants and animals. Today, they can be found underground. Companies drill deep underground to find pockets of liquid oil and gases, such as methane. They build huge oil wells to pump out the oil and gas. Many oil wells are located on the sea bed. Coal is dug out from between layers of rock in mines.

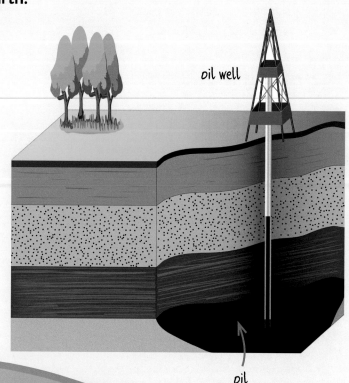

oil well

oil

Uses

Fossil fuels are commonly burned in power plants to generate electricity. The burning fuel produces heat, which is used to boil water. The boiling water makes steam, which is used to turn a turbine. The moving turbine powers a generator, which produces electricity. Oil can also be made into petrol for cars and other vehicles, or processed into plastic.

41 per cent of electricity is currently produced by coal-fired power plants.

electricity production

plastics

fuel for vehicles

22

Greenhouse gases

Burning oil and coal produces carbon dioxide, which is a greenhouse gas. Methane (found underground and produced by animals) and water vapour (steam) are also greenhouse gases. Greenhouse gases gather in the atmosphere. They trap heat from the Earth and stop it from escaping into space. This makes the temperature on Earth increase.

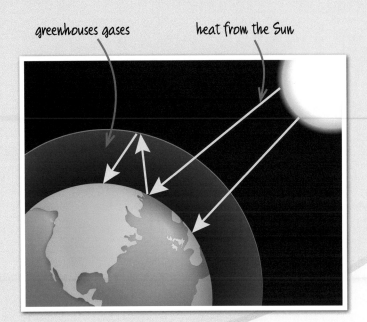

greenhouses gases

heat from the Sun

Global warming

The increase in the temperature on Earth is known as global warming. Global warming is affecting Earth's climate and weather. Some areas are experiencing drier weather. This makes it harder for people to grow enough food. The ice at the poles is melting in the warm weather. The melted water released into the ocean is making the sea level rise. Many places are at risk of flooding.

16 of the 17 warmest years on record have happened since 2001.

The edge of this melting glacier in Antarctica is falling into the sea.

! Earth's climate does naturally go through warmer and cooler periods. However, 97 per cent of scientists agree that the current climate change is due to human activity.

Acid rain

Burning fossil fuels also releases acidic chemicals that mix with water in the atmosphere and fall to the ground as acid rain. Acid rain poisons lakes, rivers and forests and can kill the animals that live in these habitats.

Renewable Energy

Renewable sources of energy, such as the wind, water and sunlight, will probably never run out. They can be used to generate large amounts of electricity over a long period of time. Some renewable energy sources are also clean energy sources, which do not release any carbon dioxide or pollution into the atmosphere.

Sunlight

Solar energy is produced by solar panels, which convert light from the Sun into electricity. People can use several small solar panels to produce electricity for their homes. Huge fields of giant panels in sunny places can generate electricity to power factories and cities. However, there are several drawbacks, including the high cost and need for sunny, bright weather.

! The amount of sunlight that hits the Earth in one hour could provide enough energy for the world to live on for one year.

Wind

When the wind moves the sails on a wind turbine, the spinning movement powers a generator that generates electricity. Some people use individual wind turbines to power their homes or businesses. Most wind turbines are placed in large groups called wind farms. Wind farms are usually built at sea or in isolated places, so that the noise they create does not bother people.

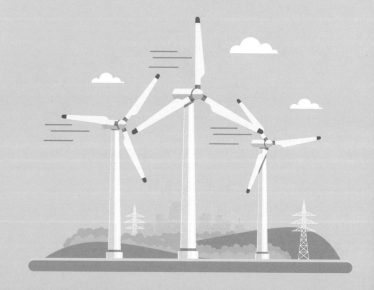

Water

The movement of water can be used to generate electricity. As water moves through a dam or because of waves or tides, it can spin a turbine. Like in wind power, this turbine powers a generator, which generates electricity. However, water turbines can destroy the habitats of water animals and plants.

The falling water in this dam powers a hydroelectric power plant.

Biomass

This energy source is made from rotting plants or animal waste. Biomass can be burned to produce heat or to power machines that generate electricity. It can even be mixed with chemicals to produce fuel for vehicles. Biomass is a renewable energy source because plants can be regrown quickly and easily. However, the burning of biomass releases carbon dioxide and other polluting gases, which makes it a less environmentally friendly option.

Geothermal energy

In volcanic areas, the natural heat of the Earth can be used to generate electricity. This is known as geothermal energy. To generate energy, water is sent underground, where it is heated by magma and becomes steam. This steam can be used to heat buildings or power a turbine to generate electricity.

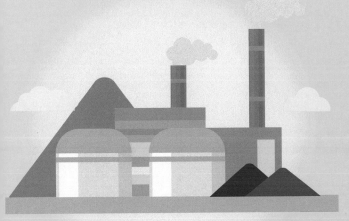

Rubbish and Recycling

Every day, we create a huge amount of waste in our homes and in factories. Finding ways to reduce and recycle rubbish helps us to use fewer resources and keep our planet clean.

Landfill

Most of the rubbish that we produce is buried in large holes in the ground, called landfill sites. The rubbish in landfill sites is usually a mixture of food waste, plastic, tins, glass and broken objects. Most of this waste will stay in the ground for thousands of years before it breaks down. Some waste also releases dangerous chemicals that poison the soil.

This worker is dumping rubbish on a landfill site in Italy.

Plastics

Plastic is a versatile material that we use in many ways, from bags and boxes to pens and furniture. Most of the plastic products that we use end up in landfill or in the ocean. Plastic in the ocean pollutes ocean habitats and kills ocean animals.

Every year, we throw away enough plastic to circle the Earth **four times.**

Biodegradable waste

Food, plant and animal waste is biodegradable. This means that it will quickly break down into soil. Some people collect their food waste to make into compost for their garden. In other places, the local council collects people's food waste from their doors. Separating biodegradable waste from the main rubbish helps to reduce the amount of waste that goes to landfill.

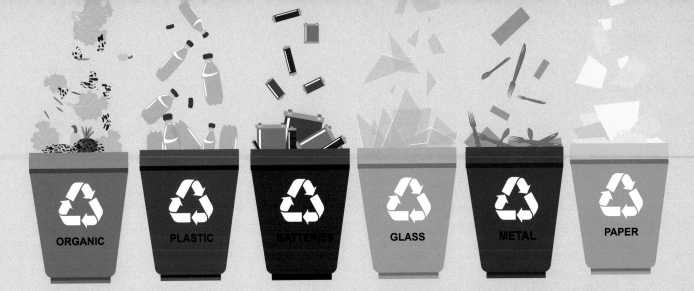

ORGANIC   PLASTIC   BATTERIES   GLASS   METAL   PAPER

Recycling

Many materials can be recycled, including glass, paper, plastic, cardboard and metal. Some people sort their recyclable waste themselves, by putting it into different recycling bins. In other places, waste is sorted by hand in large factories. Recycling plants can use magnets to separate different metals.

Energy and recycling

Recycling materials does require some electricity and can release greenhouse gases. However, recycling materials always uses less energy than making new materials from scratch.

Recycling plastic uses **70 per cent** less energy than making new plastic.

Some parts of electronic devices can be recycled. This man is separating recyclable parts at an electronic recycling plant in Turkey.

Reducing waste

It's much easier to reduce the amount of waste that you create than to recycle waste. You can use a reusable bag to carry your shopping, rather than buying disposable plastic bags. Buying fruit and vegetables without plastic packaging is another way to reduce waste.

Nuclear waste

Nuclear power plants use radioactive materials to generate energy. This process produces dangerous, radioactive waste. If this waste is placed in the ground, it poisons the soil and water and can kill living things. Nuclear waste must be buried deep underground or in a concrete case to stop it from damaging the environment.

FOCUS ON

Eco-cities

Eco-cities are cleverly planned and built to use fewer resources in a sustainable way. A large number of people can live in an eco-city without having a negative impact on the environment.

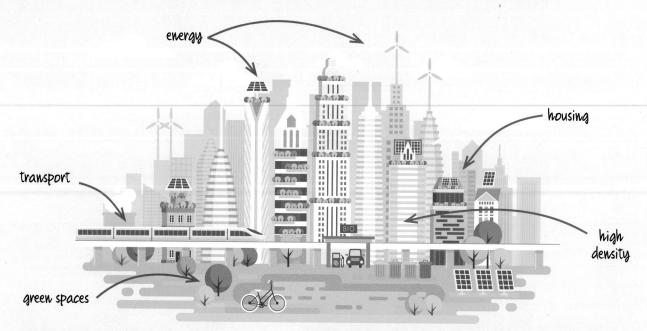

energy

housing

transport

high density

green spaces

Old and new

Many eco-cities are old cities that are gradually adapting to become more environmentally friendly. The city of Freiburg in Germany has become an eco-city by building solar power plants, improving its public transport system and helping people to recycle. In some places, they have the opportunity to build new eco-cities from scratch. Many newly built Chinese eco-cities have excellent public transport links, eco-friendly housing and green industries from the start.

This is a model of the Tianjin eco-city, which is currently under construction in China. It will eventually be home to 250,000 people and should be finished by the year 2020.

Housing

Building eco-friendly houses helps residents to use less energy. If houses are well insulated, people won't need to use as much gas and electricity for heating and cooling. Some houses have water systems that recycle used water to flush toilets. Others have solar panels to generate their own electricity.

Transport

Cars are not an environmentally friendly transport option, as most run on fossil fuels and produce air pollution. Instead, eco-cities invest in public transport links, such as trains and trams. Some trains and trams run on electricity, which means that they do not release pollution. Walking and cycling are the greenest forms of transport. Many eco-cities build cycle paths to encourage their residents to use their bikes.

There are tram services and over 500 km of cycle paths in the eco-city of Freiburg, Germany.

Waste

Eco-cities can set up recycling schemes to help their residents reduce waste. In some cities, recyclables, such as paper and tins, are collected from homes and businesses. Food waste is also collected and made into compost to fertilise farms.

High density

Eco-cities are often densely populated and have a lot of people living in a small area. This helps the city to be more environmentally friendly and consume fewer resources. It takes less energy and building supplies to build and maintain one block of flats than multiple large houses. If cities are small, it's also easier for residents to commute to their jobs by public transport or on foot.

Energy

Eco-cities aim to get as much electricity as possible from sustainable and environmentally friendly energy sources, such as solar, wind or tidal power. This reduces pollution and the amount of greenhouse gases released. The construction of new solar, wind or tidal power plants provides jobs for local residents, which is good for the economy.

Green spaces

Although eco-cites can be densely populated, it's also important for city planners to include parks and other green areas where wildlife can live. Plants absorb carbon dioxide, which helps to keep the air clean. Urban farms, built inside the city, provide food for residents. Food from local farms is cheaper and better for the environment, as it does not need to be transported by lorry.

Glossary

biodegradable describes something that will quickly break down naturally

biodiversity the number of species of plants and animals in an area

carbon dioxide a gas that is made by burning carbon or breathed out by humans and animals

crust the outer layer of the Earth

deforestation when forests are cut down and not replanted

density the number of people living in an area

drought a long period when there is not enough rain and people do not have enough water

economy the money made and used by a country

ecosystem the way in which living things interact in their environment

extract to remove

fertilise to add something to the soil to make crops grow better

fossil fuel a fuel, such as coal, gas or oil, which is from under the ground

geothermal a type of energy powered by the heat from the Earth

global warming an increase in the temperature on Earth

GM crop a crop whose genes have been modified so that it grows bigger or is more resistant to pests or disease

greenhouse gas a gas that traps heat in the Earth's atmosphere

irrigate to water crops

landfill a place where rubbish is buried in the ground

livestock animals kept on a farm for their meat or other produce

logger a person who cuts down trees for wood

non-renewable describes a resource that can not be replaced once it has been used

ore a rock from which metal can be extracted

pesticide a chemical that kills mainly insects that eat plants on farms

quarry a place where stone or other materials are cut from a large hole in the ground

radioactive something that has or produces energy from the breaking up of atoms

raw not processed

renewable describes a resource that can be replaced once it has been used

reservoir an artificial lake

sap the liquid inside plants and trees

sustainable describes something that does not damage the environment and so can continue for a long time

timber wood that has been processed and cut

Test yourself!

1   Name two non-renewable resources.

2   What is the name of aluminium ore?

3   What is slash and burn?

4   What is a cash crop?

5   What percentage of electricity in the world is currently produced by coal-fired power plants?

6   Name a greenhouse gas.

7   Where does the energy in geothermal energy come from?

8   Why is plastic in the ocean dangerous?

Check your answers on page 32.

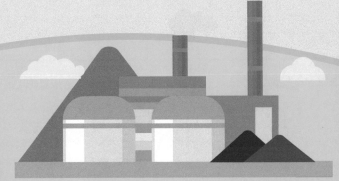

Further reading

***Source to Resource* series**
Michael Bright (Wayland, 2016)

***Eco Works* series**
Geoff Barker, Robyn Hardyman, Nick Hunter, Louise Spilsbury (Franklin Watts, 2017)

Natural Resources (The World in Infographics)
Jon Richards and Ed Simkins (Wayland, 2014)

Websites

Read more about resources at the following websites:

www.dkfindout.com/uk/earth/rocks-and-minerals/metals-from-rocks/

climatekids.nasa.gov/menu/energy/

www.sciencekids.co.nz/sciencefacts/recycling.html

Index

Answers

1. Coal, oil or minerals

2. Bauxite

3. Chopping down and then burning trees to clear space for farming

4. A crop grown to make money, rather than to provide food for a community

5. 41 per cent

6. Carbon dioxide, methane or water vapour

7. The natural heat of the Earth

8. It pollutes ocean habitats and kills ocean animals

GEOGRAPHICS
Series contents lists

Biomes
- What is a Biome? • Forests
- Yosemite • Rainforests • The Amazon Rainforest • Grasslands and Savannahs • The Serengeti
- Deserts • The Sahara Desert
- Tundra and Ice • Antarctica
- Oceans • The Great Barrier Reef
- Rivers and Lakes • The Nile River

Earthquakes
- What is an Earthquake?
- Tectonic Plates • Plate Boundaries and Faults • San Francisco 1906
- Measuring Earthquakes
- Earthquake Hazards • Peru 1970
- Earthquakes and Buildings
- Rescue and Relief • Nepal 2015
- Preparing for Earthquakes
- Tsunamis • Japan 2011

Earth's Resources
- What are Resources? • Mining
- Wood • Plastic • Recycling and Rubbish • Agriculture • GM Crops
- Fishing • North Sea Fishing
- Recycling • Fossil Fuels
- Sustainable Energy • Eco-cities

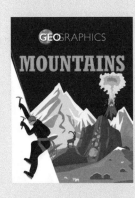

Mountains
- What is a Mountain?
- Moving Plates • Fold and Block Mountains • Volcanic Mountains
- The Andes • Changing Mountains
- The Alps • Climate • Biomes
- The Rocky Mountains • People and Mountains • The Himalayas
- Mountain Resources
- The Appalachian Mountains

Population and Settlement
- What are Population and Settlement? • Distribution and Density • Population Growth
- Overpopulation • Population Structure • Uganda and Japan
- Migration • UK Migration
- Settlement Sites • Athens
- Settlement Layout • Manila
- Changing Settlements

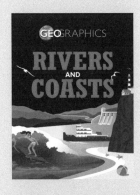

Rivers and Coasts
- Rivers and Coasts • River Structure • The Ganges River
- River Erosion • River Formations
- The Colorado River • Types of Coasts • The UK Coast • Changing Coasts • Arches and Stacks • The Twelve Apostles • People and Water • The Three Gorges Dam
- Flooding • Venice

Volcanoes
- What are Volcanoes?
- Formation • The Ring of Fire
- Stratovolcanoes • Mount Fuji
- Shield Volcanoes • Mauna Kea
- Calderas and Cinder Cones
- Eruption • Mount Vesuvius
- Lava • Underwater Volcanoes
- Dormant and Extinct Volcanoes

The Water Cycle
- What is the Water Cycle?
- Our Blue Planet • Evaporation
- The Amazon Rainforest
- Condensation • Clouds
- Precipitation • Rainfall • Rain in the Himalayas • Accumulation
- River Basins • The Mississippi River
- Water Stores • Polar Ice Caps
- Humans and the Water Cycle